THE COMPLETE GUIDE TO SPRING TRAINING 2025 / ARIZONA

KEVIN REICHARD

**August
Publications**

CONTENTS

The Complete Guide to Spring Training 2025 / Arizona

August Publications
215 10th Av. S., Unit 621
Minneapolis, MN 55415
augustpublications.com

ISBN 978-1-938532-84-9 (Print)
ISBN 978-1-938532-85-6 (eBook)

9 8 7 6 5 4 3 2 1

Designer (cover): Natalie Nowytski

ACKNOWLEDGMENTS

After spending a huge chunk of time in Arizona for spring training in March 2024, one thing is abundantly clear: We are back to normal. Yes, the three springs between 2020 and 2023 were rough, but after meeting fans, front-office folks, and players last spring, it's time to relax and welcome what should be a great time in 2025.

For those of us attending spring training in 2021-2024, this book is for us, the true believers. We find spring-training attendees to be among the most unique in all of baseball because of their unbridled optimism for everything related to America's Pastime. This book is dedicated to those hearty souls who plan their vacations around a trip to spring training, saving up for a week of travel throughout Arizona.

No matter what obstacle is placed in their path, spring-training fans arrive in Arizona with tubes of sunscreen and big smiles. And in these times, they're rewarded with a return to normalcy. This book is for you.

Thanks go to the readers of *Spring Training Online*, the Internet gathering spot for the true spring-training fans detailed above. Thanks go to my family: my wife, Courtney, and my kids, Sean, Rachel, and Sarah, who find themselves being dragged to every manner of ballpark big and small all spring and summer long.

—Kevin Reichard
July 2024

WARM BREEZES, COLD BEER, SUNNY SKIES

People ask me what I do in the winter when there's no baseball. I'll tell you what I do. I stare out the window and wait for spring.—Rogers Hornsby

No news is usually the best news. For teams and fans, spring training 2024 was free of drama: No schedule delays, no canceled games, no natural disasters impacting game schedules. The only news was generated on the field—not in the stands or the front office.

In 2024, the things we love about spring training—the player access, the fun food offerings, the intimacy of games in smaller ballparks—returned. Some of the game changes we saw after the COVID shutdown continued, such as paperless ticketing and contactless concessions. These changes to spring training were accelerated by but ultimately made inevitable thanks to the evolution of ballpark technology.

This is great news. Because, as we all know, there's no better time of year than spring training in Phoenix. From that first flight into Sky Harbor Airport to that first view of Camelback Mountain to that first pitch on the initial day of workouts, a day during Cactus League season is truly a day to remember.

Spring training is America's annual transformation from darkness to light, from cold to warm, when millions of baseball fans—both hardcore and casual—descend upon warmer climes to shed their winter blues. It's especially true for those of us in cold-weather climes like Seattle, Denver, or Chicago. Baseball's spring training is not a luxury but a necessity, our reward for living in climates filled with overcast skies, snow, ice, and rain.

Beer and brats in hand, we arrive at Arizona spring-training games every February and March to soak up some sun and catch some baseball. We wait months for that first whiff of freshly mown grass at the ballpark, that first foul ball, that first inevitable sunburn. Who cares whether the starting pitcher is some kid who will likely begin the season as a Double-A Rocket City Trash Panda? So long as the drinks are cold and the dogs are hot, all is right with the world.

We begin planning our winter getaways months in advance, juggling airline schedules and hotel openings to ensure the maximum number of games. We show up to morning workouts just to stand by the fences and feel like we're part of the action. We slather ourselves with sunscreen while waiting in line to enter Tempe Diablo Stadium or Camelback Ranch. And we take spring-training performances a lot more seriously than do many players and managers.

This book is both for the hardcore baseball fan scouting out their favorite team in depth and the more casual fan heading to spring training in search of the perfect suntan. In fact, the casual fan is more likely to get something out of this book. While the hardcores just want to know the shortest route between their hotel and the ballpark, the casual fan knows that the richness of spring training is augmented with visits to local restaurants, shopping areas, and area attractions. It is a total experience, not merely a search for a phenom's autograph.

Spring training in Arizona is a concentrated affair, where 15 teams train in the greater Phoenix area at just 10 facilities.

This concentration makes for baseball nirvana, as you can hit many games with relatively little fuss. (Time it right and you can experience five straight days of doubleheaders, as we did in recent years.) A spring-training game in Tempe, Scottsdale, or Peoria tends to be a rowdier affair, with kids romping through the outfield berm and college students letting off some steam. Florida is your father's spring training, and Arizona is a party.

INSIDER'S TIP
If you're one of those people who goes to spring training both in Florida and Arizona, you may want to check out the Florida edition of *The Complete Guide to Spring Training*. It's available via the August Publications website, *amazon.com*, *bn.com* and the Apple Bookstore.

We've arranged this book by ballpark, in alphabetical order: American Family Fields of Phoenix (Milwaukee Brewers), Camelback Ranch-Glendale (Chicago White Sox, Los Angeles Dodgers), Goodyear Ballpark (Cincinnati Reds, Cleveland Guardians), Hohokam Stadium (The Athletics), Peoria Stadium (San Diego Padres, Seattle Mariners), Salt River Fields at Talking Stick (Arizona Diamondbacks, Colorado Rockies), Scottsdale Stadium (San Francisco Giants), Sloan Park (Chicago Cubs), Surprise Stadium (Kansas City Royals, Texas Rangers), and Tempe Diablo Stadium (Los Angeles Angels). We also include information about areas outside of Arizona where spring-training games are held, such as Las Vegas, as well as college facilities in the area. Plan your time well and you can see a lot of baseball in a short amount of time.

What can we expect in 2025? Expect players to report around Feb. 12 or so, with exhibition and Cactus League games beginning Feb. 20 and the regular season launching March 27. The Dodgers and the Cubs will be reporting for camp even earlier—the first week of February—as the pair will begin the 2025 MLB season on March 18 in Tokyo. (Yes, the eBook version will be updated as schedules are updated, and the updated eBook will be a free download if you buy the eBook from August Publications or Amazon.) For up-to-the-minute information, check out *springtrainingonline.com*.

When it comes to restaurants and attractions, things can change quickly. The listings here were current as of August 2024. In past editions, there were plenty of situations where a restaurant or bar we listed went out of business by the time this book was released. And despite to a return to normalcy, today's economic climate is far from normal, so we're seeing some restaurants and shops go out of business—but, on the flip side, we're seeing plenty of new businesses open as well. When in doubt, check this book's website, *springtrainingonline.com*, for up-to-the-minute information.

And don't forget there's a normal amount of change between each spring-training season as well, with baseball teams implementing changes from season to season. Quite often there are small changes to spring-training venues in terms of food, drink, and parking, with the upgrades announced right before spring training begins. We do our best to track these changes, but given the deadlines of book publishing, we obviously can't include them all in this book. The best place to keep track of the changes in spring training is in our twice-weekly Spring Training Online newsletter. You can sign up for a free subscription at *springtrainingonline.com*.

SPRING TRAINING: AN AMERICAN TRADITION

We live in an increasingly crowded sports marketplace, but one thing remains constant: the appeal of low-tech, low-stress spring training. Many fans consider spring training to be the best time in the baseball season. While the ballparks are modern and pitchers have stopped running wind sprints in the outfield, spring training is still a celebration of everything that is right with baseball.

Spring training has remained a cornerstone activity for baseball fans hardcore and casual, though it has certainly changed over the years. In the not-too-distant past, spring training could be attended on a whim, with plenty of good seats available at the gate and fewer than a thousand fans in the stands. Those days are long gone and, in this age of fans seeking great experiences of all sorts, spring training has exploded in popularity over the last 20 years.

How popular is spring training? Attendance has been down the last few years, as you might expect. Overall, 7,345 fans per game were on hand for spring-training games in Arizona, Florida, and Las Vegas in 2024, up from 7,026 fans per game played on a limited schedule in 2022. Yes, more on approaching normalcy: In 2019, the last "normal" spring training, 7,623 fans per game attended spring training in Arizona, Florida, and Las Vegas.

According to the Seidman Research Institute at Arizona State University's W.P. Carey School of Business, spring training 2023 generated $710.2 million in overall economic impact for the Phoenix area. The *Wall Street Journal* estimated that spring training generates some $1.3 billion in spending in a normal run.

Spring training, obviously, is a big deal.

THE PLANNING PROCESS

Though the beginning of spring training marks the official start of the baseball season, teams prepare for training camp months in advance. Planning starts at the end of the prior season, when team equipment managers start laying in supplies in advance of spring training, and team officials release spring-training schedules.

Truck Day is now regarded by many as the unofficial launch to spring training. In late January and early February, each team ships its equipment from its home ballpark to its spring-training site. Most MLB teams have turned this rather mundane shipment into a full-fledged event, flooding social media with photos of trucks being loaded, leaving the ballpark, and arriving at the spring-training facility. Several teams have even sold naming rights to the event.

We're talking some serious shipments here. In 2024, here's what the Milwaukee Brewers shipped to American Family Fields of Phoenix:

- 20,500 baseballs
- 1,000 bats
- 500 pairs of socks
- 250 pairs of batting gloves
- 200 batting helmets
- 200 official spring training game jerseys
- 300 pairs of pants
- 500 pairs of socks
- 5 racing sausages
- Bob Uecker's radio booth chair and mic

Spring training now requires a certain level of planning from fans as well. Timeshares and hotels must be reserved, relatives must be warned, vacations must be requested, and school schedules must be consulted. We understand. It can be difficult at times to plan for spring training. In this chapter, we'll go through the steps needed to prepare for your spring travels.

At all times, you can catch schedules both permanent and tentative at *springtrainingonline.com*.

INSIDER'S TIP
We do a Spring Training Online newsletter, and we send out issues when schedules are updated. It's free, and you can sign up at *springtrainingonline.com*.

PLANNING YOUR TRIP

There are three ways to approach a visit to spring training: for games, for workouts, or for both. We love doing both—workouts in the morning, a game in the afternoon—but there are plenty of folks who focus on games as their spring-training experience.

The first thing to do from the comfort of your easy chair is budgeting a trip. Research from the Seidman Institute on 2023 may provide you with some budgeting assistance. According to their research, the average Cactus League out-of-town visitor stays four nights and attends three games, spending $421.25 per day. So plan accordingly.

For many, spring training begins when it does for players: on reporting day, this year in the middle of February (think Valentine's Day). Decades ago, that first reporting day was a big deal. Players were reentering the baseball world from their offseason jobs, and they were subject to a physical, a weigh-in, and a general evaluation by team officials. With players mostly out of touch between October and February, there were always some surprises on reporting day, mostly of the unpleasant kind, when a player should show up fat and out of shape.

For today's baseball player, the game is a full-time job. The days of Willie Aikens dropping thirty-plus pounds in spring training to make the California Angels as a rookie are long gone. Virtually every player trains in the offseason or plays winter ball, and organizations keep close tabs on most players, especially the well-paid prospects and superstars. Very few surprises come that first reporting date, as many players have already been hanging out around training facilities for several weeks or months.

Many fans like to show up for those first practices, as they're a great way to get close to the players as they run through drills. Many practice areas are set up for fan comfort, with shaded seating and even concessions. There are some big rewards to showing up for workouts: players tend to be accessible at those initial workouts and more willing to sign autographs after practice. We cover every team's practice schedule individually online; there's no uniform MLB schedule to practices, and every team sets its own start time and location. (We update them on *springtrainingonline.com* as further information is released.) The actual workout period is quite short, running the 10 days or so from pitcher/catcher reporting dates (Feb. 12-14) to the first game, when the schedule changes.

INSIDER'S TIP
Practices are organized, and while MLB teams have added many creature comforts to workout facilities, they don't feel compelled to share their organizational plan with you. You're welcome to observe from a respectful distance—either in the stands in the main ballpark or somewhere next to the practice field—and teams are very explicit about where you're allowed to watch. Many teams rope off access to specific areas of the training complex at certain times. At the end of the day, the attitude from MLB teams is that practices are for players, not for fans.

Another thing regarding practice schedules: teams have general times for workouts, but the specifics will vary from day to day. They aren't posted online, and they aren't released to the public. Some teams will post morning practice updates on their Instagram accounts, but the practice is hardly uniform in the baseball world.

Cactus League games begin on Feb. 21 and run through March 23, with exhibitions slated for March 24-25. As has been the case in previous years, the MLB schedule will begin with a foreign series, in this case the Los Angeles Dodgers and Chicago Cubs playing a pair of games in Seoul, March 18-19. Both teams will be reporting to spring training early and ending spring training games early.

When games begin, workouts are curtailed. Most teams

will gather in the morning for workouts, but the real focus is the afternoon game. You can show up early and see who you can catch at the morning workout. (Indeed, that's one of the big advantages of a modern spring facility like Camelback Ranch-Glendale or Salt River Fields: they are designed to bring fans close to practice areas before they ever hit the ball-park.) Conversely, if a team is on the road, the regulars not scheduled for the trip will often work out in the morning during a regularly scheduled workout time.

In fact, this emphasis on games versus long workouts designed to sweat the booze out of out-of-shape players is perhaps the biggest shift in the modern age of spring training. Most players come to spring training in shape, so the need for intense physical workouts is mitigated. Most teams have their basic rosters set weeks before spring training—but some roster spots are still won and lost during spring training. Take, for example, 2017 phenom Aaron Judge. When the New York Yankees were close to breaking camp in 2017, the front office had not yet decided on whether to keep Judge on the roster or send him to Triple-A Scranton/Wilkes-Barre. In the end, the Yankees went with Judge in right field, and the rest was history. Now, Judge's case is a little unusual in that most teams have an idea of their Opening Day lineup well before camp breaks. Indeed, for most teams, the last week of spring training is to determine the last two pitchers in the bullpen, the fifth outfielder should a team carry five, a potential third catcher, etc.

So why go to practices? Eagerness to begin the season. Enthusiasm for the upcoming campaign. Desire to snare an autograph.

Though you'll find plenty of fans milling around camp after players report, the real action starts when games begin at the end of February and early March. This, for most fans, is the real beginning of spring training. And although the

SPRING TRAINING: AN AMERICAN TRADITION

starting lineups during those first few weeks of games will bear little resemblance to the Opening Day lineup, enough stars will be present to make those games worthwhile. In general, you'll need a long lineup card to keep track of all the players shuttling on and off the field for those games. Technically, any team playing on the road is required by Major League Baseball to feature four regulars from the previous season (and yes, it's defined: position players must have recorded at least 300 at-bats in the prior season) in the lineup, but not every team strictly hews to that requirement. Pitchers are restricted by pitch and inning counts, starters are limited to just three or four innings on the field, and by the seventh inning you'll be watching mostly players already ticketed for time at the Triple-A or Double-A levels.

So what? You're out in the sun at a glorious time of year partaking in America's Pastime. It's a great experience no matter if you're watching a starting MLB pitcher or a kid destined (in the short-term, at least) to be an Amarillo Sod Poodle.

One more thing to note when scheduling your time: most spring-training games are played in the afternoon. Some teams do not schedule any night games; others will schedule several. In the Cactus League, any night game is a bonus. Some teams, like the Milwaukee Brewers, don't even schedule night games. So be grateful when you can create your own doubleheader. The relatively short distances between ballparks assures that a hardcore spring-training fan can easily take in two games in one day, and with both Arizona State University and Grand Canyon University playing a full slate of night games, it's very easy to set up a day-night doubleheader for the serious baseball fan.

HOW TO ORDER TICKETS

There's no one date when all MLB teams put spring-training tickets on sale: each team sets a sale date separately, some-times with very little warning. Most teams put tickets on sale in January. Some, like Milwaukee and the Athletics, will usually put tickets on sale in December, while other teams will put tickets on sale in early February.

Unless you are lucky enough to score tickets the day they go on sale or buy a season ticket, you'll need to order them later from teams and deal with the distinct possibility that popular games are sold out. Many of you will hit the resale market—not the worst outcome.

Buying your ticket directly from the team will usually be the cheapest way to snare a ducat. With popular teams, the selection will be limited. Every team sells spring-training season tickets, bought mostly by locals and snowbirds, and the best tickets in any spring ballpark are controlled by these season-ticket holders. Indeed, MLB teams have put an emphasis on building a season-ticket base, cutting down the number of tickets available for any single game. Many of the best tickets to a game at a Salt River Fields or Scottsdale Stadium have been sold for weeks before single-game seats go on sale, as season-ticket holders control the top inventory.

Still, tickets are available from a variety of sources. Most people assume that only MLB teams sell tickets, but that's not the case. MLB teams do sell most spring-training tickets, but there are usually some alternative ways to come up with ducats for a popular match.

For sheer convenience, however, your search for tickets should begin with the MLB teams. They're set up best to sell massive amounts of tickets in a short amount of time. The beginning of spring-training ticket sales can best be described as a feeding frenzy, as tens of thousands of fans rush to obtain tickets for specific games.

There are four ways to order spring-training tickets directly from MLB teams: via telephone, via the Internet, in person, and via the U.S. Mail. We'll describe each.

- **Via the Internet.** The vast majority of spring-training tickets are now sold on the Internet. There are some pluses and minuses to this approach. On the one hand, you can bypass clogged phone lines and make your purchases directly, although Ticketmaster has implemented the equivalent of telephone wait times when you buy popular tickets online. New ticketing systems are sophisticated: many teams have systems where you can order specific seats or see a list of available seats within a section and select the ones you want. And yes, you'll also pay a ticketing fee for the convenience of buying tickets. But by using a credit card online you are able to receive an instant refund if a game is canceled: you don't even need to call in.

- **Via telephone.** Many tickets are sold via phone sales. This can be a frustrating way of doing things, as you're likely to encounter some busy signals or long wait times when tickets first go on sale. Don't bother calling before the tickets are technically on sale: all you'll do is waste your time and irritate the ticket reps. They can't help you until the tickets are on sale; no, they can't cut you a paper ticket; they won't call you back; and they won't put you on a secret list to be hauled out when tickets are on sale. When the tickets do go on sale—and you'll find a complete listing of when tickets go on sale at the *springtrainingonline.com* team pages—be prepared to call early in the day for popular games, like the A's-Giants matchups. You'll also pay a ticketing fee for the convenience of buying tickets.

- **In person.** Most teams let you order spring-training tickets at their main ticket office at the major-league ballpark or local team stores. The Colorado

Rockies, for example, sell spring-training tickets at the Denver-area Rockies Dugout Stores. There are three big advantages to buying tickets in person: you can usually get a good idea of the range of available tickets, you can request specific seats, and you won't need to wait too long in line. Plus, the major-league and spring-training box offices are the only locations where you won't incur handling fees. One troubling trend we are seeing: many teams first put tickets on sale via online and phone sales and then don't open the spring-training box office until several weeks have passed by, some not until the team's reporting date. The days when tickets went on sale locally and online simultaneously are long gone. Alas, you won't be able to avoid electronic tickets in person: you'll choose the dates and seats, hand over a credit card for payment, and then receive an email with instructions on how to download the tickets to the MLB Ballpark App.

- **Via U.S. Mail**. Some teams let you order tickets via the mail. You send in your money for a certain price range, and you take whatever tickets the team decides to send you. Will you receive the best tickets in your price range? Depends on the whims of a ticket rep with the team. The advantage, however, is that these orders tend to be filled first, so you are virtually assured of receiving tickets to the game of your choice.

INSIDER'S TIP
Despite the move to etickets, paper tickets have not totally disappeared, though MLB teams are doing their best to guide fans to electronic tickets and the MLB

Ballpark App. (Yes, that means you will need an email address to register an account on the app.) If you order tickets and plan on picking them up at the ballpark at Will Call, make sure you have the confirmation number and an ID with you. Ticket-office personnel are instructed to make sure that the right person is picking up tickets. More than once have we waited in the Will Call line and cooled our heels while the party in front of us argues in vain with the ticket staff over disputed tickets. In general, the Will Call folks are pretty accommodating. You can leave tickets there for other members of your group at no charge even if not purchased directly from the team, letting you enter the ballpark instead of waiting at the front gates for your friends.

INSIDER'S TIP

The current trend is toward paperless tickets, billed as a safety measure by many teams to prevent contact between a worker and a fan. This is somewhat disingenuous—teams use scanners at the gates, and it makes no difference if you're scanning in a bar code on a piece of paper or a phone screen—but paperless tickets do give MLB teams more control over tickets, and they certainly like control. But you can buy e-tickets anywhere on the aftermarket, and they'll work just fine.

In recent years, you could count on tickets being on sale at the spring-training offices in Florida or Arizona. Generally, this is still true, but not every spring box office opens when tickets go on sale. These days many teams offer tickets for sale at the launch of sales season only online and via the phone. Weeks later, the sales office at the spring-training site would open for business and stay open through the start of spring training. Each team does it differently, and we note the specific dates and locations on *springtrainingonline.com* when they are released by MLB teams.

Teams also offer two more ways to obtain tickets that may fit your needs.

If you think you'll be attending many games, consider a season ticket. Season-ticket packages go on sale weeks before single-game tickets. Usually season tickets are the province of locals and brokers, but if you really, really want some tix for the Athletics-Giants games and realize that you have no chance of obtaining a good ticket via conventional means, spring for the season ticket and then try to sell tickets to some of the other games via eBay or StubHub.

Other teams offer a break to groups of 10 or more. Again, this won't apply if just you and your friends or family are heading to a game, but there may be opportunities where you could put together a group (via a church organization, an Internet chat site, etc.) that could buy discounted tickets to a game or two. These transactions require some interaction with a sales agent. At this time no team is offering discounted group tickets online during the course of spring training; you'll need to contact the sales office and talk to a human.

INSIDER'S TIP

If you can, schedule a game on St. Patrick's Day. It's the only real holiday celebrated at the spring-training ballpark, and most teams do something to mark the occasion, whether it be green uniforms or food specials. You can also bet watering holes close to the ballparks will have some St. Patrick's Day drink specials as well. In 2025, St. Patrick's Day falls on a Monday, making for the end of an extended baseball weekend.

BUYING AT THE GATE

The nice thing about the Internet is that you can gauge ticket availability even if you have no intention of buying a ducat online. At some of the bigger spring ballparks, there's no chance of a game selling out. So you can roll the dice and buy your tickets at the gate. As a bonus, the ballpark ticket office is the place where you can take advantage of a senior discount. They're not offered by all teams, but we do note on *springtrainingonline.com* where they are offered. The same goes for military discounts: some teams offer them, some do not. So if you're willing to take a chance on your seat location, by all means buy tickets at the gate. We don't recommend it (we like to know where we are sitting before we leave home and rest easy knowing we'll be able to get into the game), but feel free to live dangerously.

WORKING WITH THIRD-PARTY RESELLERS

There is another way to obtain a single-game ticket: through a third-party reseller. Resellers used to be anathema to the baseball industry, until teams realized resellers should be embraced and encouraged—to an extent. Today every MLB team embraces the open market with official ticket partners that end up offering ducats through other resellers. They also put tickets on sale early, giving you peace of mind in your planning process. They're also not shy about telling the world about the availability of the tickets, so if you want to go to a game badly enough, chances are good one of them will step up with a ticket. (The newest trend in the broker world: as teams do, they offer downloadable electronic tickets.) We work with a very reputable vendor to offer tickets at *ballparkdigesttickets.com*; of course, we'd recommend you start there. In 2024, we saw the market at work: tickets for early season Boston Red Sox games sold far below face value because the season-ticket holders wanted to attend games later in March, not in early February. (Generally, the first 10 days of spring training is the best period for scoring a cheaper aftermarket ticket.) And by using a credit card online with a broker you are able to receive an instant refund if a game is canceled: you don't even need to call in.

WHERE TO STAY

If you lack friends or family in Arizona, you'll need to arrange housing for your stay. There are a few ways to go.

The obvious choice is a hotel. Every spring-training site in the Phoenix area is in an urban or suburban area and features easy access to a slew of hotels. You'll pay more to stay near the more popular ballparks; in our guides to each venue we list the closest hotels to each ballpark and tell you if it's worth staying nearby. (In many cases, it's not, but in a few cases, such as with hotels in downtown Scottsdale, you'll appreciate the convenience of proximity to Scottsdale Stadium.) There are some baseball fanatics who insist on staying within walking distance of a spring-training facility, but they a) tend to spend the entire day at the facility and b) don't want to spring for the cost of a car.

In the chapters covering specific complexes, we list the local numbers for hotels located close to the ballparks, as well as the official hotel for every team. Yes, fans—not just base-ball Annies—still hang around hotel lobbies hoping for a glimpse of a star or a potential autograph opportunity. You won't be alone.

Hotel rates have soared in the greater Phoenix area driving spring training, so there's a chance you could be shut out of an affordable hotel room for spring training—if you're not flexible about where you stay. There are many hotels in

Scottsdale catering to the spring-training fan, but the hotels near Sky Harbor Airport cater to business travelers. In your favor, hotels tend to be scattered throughout the Valley, but usually located near some major interstate interchange or a major attraction, like State Farm Stadium or the Arizona State University campus. In general, you're never going to be too far away from any spring-training venue. Granted, there are caveats—if you're a Texas Rangers or Kansas City Royals fan, you probably don't want to stay out in Chandler or Apache Junction, on the opposite side of the Valley—but you'll probably find plenty of hotel rooms in the northwest quadrant of the Valley, in any case: in recent years we've seen a lot of new hotels opening in the Peoria/Glendale/Surprise area.

There are some alternatives to daily-stay hotels. The most prominent is a residence-sharing service like Airbnb or VRBO, where you can see the specifics of the rental before committing. There are plenty of listings for the likes of Phoenix or Scottsdale during spring training. While they may not be the cheapest venues under the sun, you won't get that hotel feel when staying at someone else's residence. Depending on your viewpoint, that's either a good thing or a bad thing. Just beware the hidden fees: don't be sucked in by a cheap daily or weekly rate and then be surprised by a sizable cleaning fee.

There are many folks who visit spring training in the comfort of their own RV. They're the ones setting up shop three or four hours before a game, grilling their pregame brats, watching the noontime news. Though you can't park overnight at any ballpark parking lot, most communities hosting spring training also support several RV parks, and some ballparks have special areas set up for RV parking, but these are becoming more scarce as areas around ballparks are developed. The greater Phoenix market is geared toward snowbirds, and snowbirds like RVs; hence the need for RV parks. We note them throughout this book.

You don't even need to own an RV to use one for spring training: Companies like Cruise America rent RVs by the day or week from hundreds of locations across the United States. Today's RV is not like yesterday's RV. They have considerably more amenities (like showers, decent bathrooms, and air conditioning) and are more reliable than in the past. And modern RV parks can be amazingly upscale, with shaded parking, wireless networking, and more.

MAKING YOUR WAY TO THE BALLPARK: PLANES, TRAINS, AND AUTOMOBILES

Getting to the city hosting spring training is one thing. Making your way to your hotel room and the ballpark is another.

While public transit has improved in Phoenix thanks to light rail, the transit system really isn't geared to spring-training fans. (Light rail, alas, doesn't serve a single spring-training facility, although there is talk about extending a line to Sloan Park in the future.) Yes, you can rely on buses to get to many facilities, and *valleymetro.org* lists all the light-rail and bus schedules and routes. But, realistically, unless you're staying at a hotel within walking distance of a ballpark that is also adjacent to plenty of dining and shopping options (i.e., hello, downtown Scottsdale or the Talking Stick area), you'll need to resign yourself to an inevitable cost of attending spring training: paying for a car. Sure, you could rely on Uber or Lyft rides or drive your own car to spring training—and trust us, plenty of folks do just that, as evidenced by the large number of Colorado license plates in the Salt River Fields parking lot throughout March—but if you're committed to flying, some planning is required.

While the car-rental business has rebounded since COVID

impacts, it's still an expensive proposition to rent a car in Phoenix, between high rates and steep taxes.

INSIDER'S TIP
There are no car rentals at Sky Harbor Airport. They were all relocated several years ago to an offsite facility. This is more convenient than it sounds: a rail line connects the rental-car facility and the airport, making it a smooth process when picking up a rental.

INSIDER'S TIP
Consider an alternative to rental cars: ridesharing services like Uber and Lyft. The appeal: you can order a car at a specific place at a specific time, and you can be dropped off at or near the ballpark. (Most, but not every spring-training ballpark has a designated dropoff area. But any smart driver in Peoria or Tempe can get you fairly close to the ballpark.) They definitely lessen the need for a rental car for those staying in more urban areas, like Scottsdale or Peoria. You could certainly stay at a neighborhood hotel and then arrange a rideshare to and from the games.

ATTENDING A GAME: SOME GENERAL GUIDELINES

Now that you actually have a game ticket, a plane ticket, a hotel room, and a car, you're all ready to actually attend a spring-training game. Congratulations!

There are some things you should know.

- Most spring-training complexes open at least two hours before game time, and they generally run the same schedule for a 1:05 p.m. game start, which we note on team pages. (Alas, there's no uniform MLB

schedule for when workouts start.) This is usually
the best time to score autographs: players are
relaxed during their warm-ups and happy to
wander over to the stands and sign away. Or you
could head to the practice facility in the morning
and try to score some autographs there. Newer
spring-training complexes, like Salt River Fields
and Camelback Ranch-Glendale, put a premium on
player accessibility, as you can take in the workouts
before the ballpark opens for the afternoon game.
They're built to give you a chance to get up close
and personal with players and coaches in a very
pleasant atmosphere.

- Many of the ushers at spring-training games are
  volunteers, usually seniors living in the area. Don't
  hassle them: they're volunteering at games because
  they love baseball. Some of them can be a little on
  the officious side, but remember their job is to make
  sure fans are in their proper seats. In Peoria, 581
  Diamond Backers in the Peoria Diamond Club
  work Seattle and San Diego games as ushers,
  program sellers, parking-lot attendants, and more.
  In Surprise, the Sundancers help out with game-
  day operations. Hohokam Foundation volunteers
  are involved both at Hohokam Stadium and Sloan
  Park. And, of course, the Charros are an important
  part of San Francisco Giants spring training at
  Scottsdale Stadium.

- You're not always assured of seeing a superstar or
  even a famous player at a spring-training game.
  Teams are notorious for leaving their best players at
  home. There is a rule that each team must send four
  regulars on the road to play in an exhibition game,

but there's a big difference between a superstar and
a regular on many teams.

- Don't be in a hurry to leave the ballpark once a
game is done. Some coaches will hold a practice
right after an afternoon game, either in the main
ballpark or a practice field. This doesn't happen as
often as it once did, unfortunately. Another bonus
to remaining for entire games: players will usually
sign on their way back to the clubhouses.

"B" GAMES

You don't need to shell out the big bucks to see major
leaguers in action during spring training.

If you're willing to put up with missing a few creature
comforts like seatbacks, concessions, and restrooms, you can hit
a "B" game held on a satellite field in a spring-training complex.
These are pure practice games, usually held in the late morning.
There's no scoreboard tracking the action or an announcer
introducing the players, so you should know a little about the
rosters and players to get anything out of the experience.

And you can't be too much of a purist. As said, these are
true practice games: players bat out of order and wander in
and out of the lineup depending on the situation.

But these games are also excellent places to see the real
major leaguers work on their game: you're never going to be
closer to a superstar practicing one specific part of their game.
Hard-working players are legendary for using these games to
work on their swings, and pitchers will use the time to work
out the kinks on a specific pitch.

In the past, teams held "B" games almost daily, but they
seem to be going by the wayside. Call the team's local box
office in the morning to see if a "B" game is scheduled for a

given day (they are not subject to a published schedule), but your best bet may to be wander around a facility in the morning and see if there's any action on a field.

MINOR-LEAGUE GAMES

Another option during your spring-training trip: taking in a minor-league match. These games are played on satellite fields (at the spring-training complex when possible; at a larger offsite training facility if not) and are open to anyone wandering through the facility. Unlike "B" games, minor-league games are subject to a schedule: they begin a few weeks into spring training and feature all the teams in an organization taking on all the teams from another organization. For instance, the Triple-A and Double-A teams from the Kansas City Royals will host the Triple-A and Double-A teams from the Cleveland Indians at the satellite fields at the Surprise Stadium training complex, while the two Class-A teams from the Indians will host the two Class-A Royals teams at their training complex next to Goodyear Ballpark. In the minors, there are four levels of full-season teams in training camp (Triple-A, Double-A, High-A, and Single-A); if the Triple-A and Double-A teams are home, the A teams will be away, and vice versa. Again, these games are run on a casual basis, and most of the better players will be with the parent team, but they offer a very intimate view of some of tomorrow's superstars. (They are also subject to being cancelled.) Schedules for these games are released after the beginning of the year; check *springtrainingonline.com* for a complete list of minor-league schedules, or at least the schedules released by MLB parents.

INSIDER'S TIP
We've seen fewer and fewer MLB teams release MiLB

schedules over the past five years. We've also seen MLB teams arrange fewer and fewer MiLB games over the past five years, scheduling more camp days.

MLB added another layer of MiLB matches in 2024, scheduling Spring Breakout games. These games were created with the goal of showcasing future stars, with the MLB ballparks hosting a match between top prospects in a seven-inning exhibition game, either scheduled separately or with an MLB game. The tickets were affordable—$10 in many MLB ballparks—and gave fans another chance to take in some spring action, albeit with no MLB stars.

WEATHER

You can tell a spring-training rookie by their beet-red face and sunburned shoulders. If you've spent the last four months cooped up in a climate dominated by snow and ice, you're likely to do the logical thing and bask for hours on end in the warm spring sun.

Don't.

Yes, you'll hear from everyone the importance of slathering on some sunscreen before hitting your first spring game. But the advice is sound: even a mildly overcast day can scorch your skin to the painful point, and you don't want to ruin your trip with a bad sunburn. Your best bet is to bring a plastic tube of sunscreen to a spring game; you won't be able to bring a metal spray can into the ballpark, so apply sunscreen before your walk to the ballpark. If you forget, you're in luck: many Arizona spring-training facilities offer free sunscreen, usually via dispensers next to a restroom. And even if you forget and there's no free sunscreen, most team stores sell it as well. So there's no reason for you to head home with a bad sunburn.

Otherwise, you should expect good weather for your spring-training sojourn. Phoenix can still be a little chilly at night at the beginning of March, so bring a jacket for those evenings out. You can expect the weather to be sunny and warm (75 degrees or so) for most afternoon games.

WHAT CAN I BRING INTO THE BALLPARK?

Forget about bringing much into the ballpark past a medium-sized bag. There's a uniform MLB policy regarding what you can bring into a ballpark. First, everything must fit within a backpack, cooler, or bag no larger than 16 inches by 16 inches by 8 inches. (Some ballparks require clear bags, others are less officious. Diaper bags are exempted from the size requirements.) Non-alcoholic beverages must be in sealed, plastic containers. Food must be stored in sealed, clear-plastic containers. If you're carrying any sort of backpack, purse, or larger bag, you will be asked to open it up for inspection.

Most teams are pretty mellow about backpacks and oversized bags, even if you're bringing in some peanuts or snacks. The key is to have sealed water and food: it's a way to ensure you're not sneaking booze into the ballpark. Unless noted otherwise, every team in this guide conforms to these MLB guidelines.

So forget about bringing a six-pack of cans or bottles into the park. You can't bring Fido or Fluffy with you unless your dog is a certified seeing-eye or service dog. Alas, you can't bring in sunscreen unless it's in a plastic tube (no cans), so apply sunscreen in spray form in the parking area and leave it in the car.

There are also plenty of other items not allowed in a spring-training ballpark. You can't bring in lawn chairs or umbrellas, but you can bring a seat cushion or a blanket if you want to sit in the berm. In general, firearms are not allowed, even if you have a permit for concealed carry.

INSIDER'S TIP

Not every team hews to this policy. If a team does not follow this policy, we note it in the team chapter.

INSIDER'S TIP

Our strategy for keeping those bottles of water colder longer: throw them in the freezer the night before. The ice will slowly melt at the game, keeping your water nice and cold.

INSIDER'S TIP

There are now metal detectors at every gate entering a ballpark—yes, even gameday workers and journalists must enter through the metal detectors. Many ball-parks upgraded their metal detectors to newer models that didn't requite you to remove every bit of metal from your pockets. (Here's a little secret—metal detectors aren't really metal detectors, but rather density detectors, and something like a wallet with 10 or so credit cards and IDs can set them off.) The new models, installed in the name of COVID, did indeed speed up entry times to the ballpark.

WHAT IF IT RAINS?

If it rains, you'll be able to exchange your ticket for a ticket to a future game. Many teams also refund unused tickets in case of game cancellations due to weather. You will not be refunded any service fees or parking.

A SHORT HISTORY OF SPRING TRAINING

Spring training has been around almost as long as professional baseball. Boss Tweed—yes, *that* Boss Tweed—arranged for his New York Mutuals, an amateur team made up mostly of volunteer firemen with the Mutual Hook and

Ladder Company Number 1, to train in New Orleans in 1869. Yes, the Mutuals were ostensibly amateurs, but like everything with the notorious Boss Tweed, there are multiple layers to this tale. Many of the players were likely paid under the table—a good investment given how baseball's popularity was due partially to its appeal to gamblers. Winning for a team owner worked on several levels.

So spring training has been around almost as long as professional baseball. The best evidence points to professional spring training first taking place in 1870, when the Cincinnati Red Stockings and the Chicago White Stockings held organized baseball camps in New Orleans. By 1886, spring training had spread throughout professional baseball, with at least four professional teams holding a formal training camp, and *The Sporting News* lauding the development in its inaugural March 17, 1886, issue:

> The preparatory work now being done by two or three prominent clubs in the country marks one of the most sensible departures from the old rut in base-ball that has ever been made. It has always been a matter of wonder to professional and amateur athletes that men having thousands of dollars invested in a business of which so much depends on the physical condition of their men, should pay so little attention to the matter of training these people for the arduous work that was expected of them during the six months covering the championship season. Take these same men and let them put the money that they have invested in base-ball in horse-flesh. Would they dare send their horses out on a trotting or running circuit in the spring without training them....

Man is the superior animal and really needs more care

and attention than the horse. Yet for years ball players have been sent out in the spring with muscles soft and flabby, carrying from ten to twenty pounds of extra flesh, and told to "play ball." Well, they have played ball, but the games have been "yaller," and many a man has come in from a first game with a shoulder, a leg or an arm that has impaired his effectiveness for an entire season....

That season saw the Chicago White Stockings go to Hot Springs, Arkansas, for spring training, while the Philadelphia Phillies headed to Charleston, South Carolina, for some games against local talent. The White Stockings were owned and managed by Albert Spalding (the same Spalding who founded the sporting-goods firm that exists to this day), who told *The Sporting News* of his plans to literally "boil" the members of his team in Hot Springs for two weeks:

"It's a great scheme," said Mr. Spalding yesterday, leaning back in his chair and stroking his forehead. "I wonder whatever made me think of it. All the boys are enthusiastic about it and all want to go. I have written to a professor down there, and he is making arrangements to build a vat in which he can boil the whole nine at once....I boil out all the alcoholic microbes which may have impregnated the systems of these men during the winter while they have been away from me and Anson....If that don't work I'll send 'em all over to Paris and have 'em inoculated by Pasteur."

By 1901, spring training was firmly established as a baseball ritual, with most American and National League teams heading out of town so players could train (i.e., dry out) and managers could evaluate. In those days, spring training was a considerably looser affair: players would gather in a Florida, California, Texas, Arkansas, or Louisiana city, work out for several days, sweat out the winter booze, perhaps sample some of the local delights (many teams held spring training in Hot Springs, with the city's notorious gambling establishments as an inducement to report), and then make their way back to their homes while barnstorming daily against local teams.

Even so, spring training was rarely a strenuous activity in the past. Take the Cleveland Indians of the 1920s, who trained in Lakeland, Florida, at a ballpark still standing, Henley Field. Most teams worked out only once a day, either for an hour or two; the rest of the time the players were free to play golf and carouse—which many of them did. In the 1924 *Reach Guide*, Jack Ryder reported that Indians manager Tris Speaker was a firm believer in a single, brief but strenuous daily workout.

Other teams of that era were more intense. The Brooklyn Dodgers were known for their three-hour workouts, while Pat Moran, manager of the Cincinnati Reds, held 10 a.m. and 2 p.m. workouts. Ryder seemed to approve of the Reds' schedule:

> It is the observation of this writer that the policy of Manager Moran is the best of those outlined. Ball players are young men, many of them merely boys, full of pepper and anxious to work. They all enjoy the spring training after the long lay-off of the winter. They do not ask to coddled or favored with light labor. In fact, the more work they can get, provided it is not up to the point of exhaustion, the better they like it. Furthermore, the policy of two sessions a day of practice leaves the boys less time to themselves and keeps them together more, which is always a good thing for a team. They have less temptation to

get into bad habits or bad company and the younger
recruits are more apt to follow the good example set
by the veterans on the team. It must not be under-
stood that Manager Moran is a hard driver or forces
his players too far, quite the reverse. If he sees that
any one of the athletes is lazy or inclined to shirk, he
is after him at once with a sharp stick, but there are
not many such cases. In most instances, the Reds
leader has to curb the ambition of his men instead of
urging them on. This he constantly does, not allowing
any man to get an inch beyond the limit of his
strength.

Small Florida communities were suddenly known across
the nation because of the allure provided by major-league
baseball. St. Petersburg. Plant City. Orlando. Lakeland. Vero
Beach. Fort Lauderdale. Sarasota. Bradenton. Tampa. Fans are
dismayed these days when MLB teams look for new training
facilities, but the practice is not unique to today: since the
turn of the century, cities have sought to promote themselves
to tourists after building spring-training facilities and guaran-
teeing revenues to teams. Look at the cities where the Philadelphia Athletics trained between 1903 and 1914:
Jacksonville, Spartanburg (South Carolina), Shreveport,
Montgomery (Alabama), Dallas, New Orleans, Atlanta, San
Antonio, and back to Jacksonville. No more than two years
spent in a single city, and whoever made the best offer to a
team in January usually landed the spring training in March.
That pattern prevailed until World War II.

Case in point: tiny Bogalusa, Louisiana, which hosted St.
Louis Browns (predecessor to the Baltimore Orioles) spring
training in 1921. The city lured the Brownies to their fair city
with the construction of a new grandstand and inexpensive
accommodations at the Pine Tree Inn. The *Bogalusa Enterprise*

and American of March 10, 1921 reported how pleased the Brownies were with the facilities:

> "When we ask for something at the hotel," said one of the best known players in the American League, "we are not told that 'it will be looked into,' but within a shorter time than one would expect in the best hotel in America, we are served. I never saw people so hospitable in all my life, they simply go out of their way in Bogalusa to make it enjoyable for us and I know there is not a member of the team who will not leave Bogalusa with regret when we finish our training, and I also know that if it was left to the members of the team as to where we would train next spring, that it would be Bogalusa by 100 percent."

> Manager Coleman of the Terre Haute, Ind., team of the Central League, and former manager of the Mobile club, said that the club house built here for the Browns was by far better than any club house on the American League circuit and that it passed Detroit, which had the best in the league. "The grounds," said Mr. Coleman, "are great and by next year they can be made as good as any in the country."

All of this, apparently, was not enough: the Brownies never returned to Bogalusa for spring training, heading in 1922 for Mobile, Alabama.

The first arrival of Major League Baseball in Arizona came in 1909, when the Chicago White Sox took on the local lads of Yuma while barnstorming their way back from spring training in California. As noted, in those days spring training was a completely different affair: teams would spend a few weeks at a training site and then barnstorm their way back to the Opening Day ballpark. Over the next 30 years, you would have teams training in California—the Chicago Cubs, the Pittsburgh Pirates, and the aforementioned White Sox—and then stopping off in Arizona to take on local teams.

The first MLB team to officially hold spring training in Arizona was the Detroit Tigers. In 1929, the Tigers trained at Phoenix Riverside Park and scheduled several exhibition games against local squads. The Arizona tenure was not a financial success, and in 1930 the Tigers trained in California.

An early home to spring training in Phoenix was the original Phoenix Municipal Stadium, located at Central Avenue and Mohave Street. It was built in 1937, funded by the federal Works Progress Administration. It hosted several levels of Minor League Baseball—the Phoenix Senators of the old Class C Arizona-Texas League, the Phoenix Stars of the old Class C Arizona-Mexico League, and the original Phoenix Giants of the Class AAA Pacific Coast League—as well as New York Yankees spring training (1951) and New York Giants spring training (1947-1950, 1952-1963).

When the original Phoenix Municipal Stadium opened, Central Avenue and Mohave Street wasn't exactly the middle of town: the ballpark was surrounded by farmland and limited housing. This was where the New York Giants originally trained in 1947, after Horace Stoneham shifted spring operations from the East Coast. It was in use until 1964, when the new Municipal Stadium opened. (We cover it more in-depth in our chapter on Arizona State University baseball.)

Each team has a unique spring-training history, and we present some of the highlights in each team chapter. There was one period in spring training that bears further discussion, however: spring training during the war years. We all associate spring training with warmer climes, but there was a period when major-league teams trained close to home. Travel restrictions during World War II kept teams north of the Ohio River and east of the Mississippi River; the St. Louis Browns and Cardinals were exempted and trained in the greater St. Louis area.

As a result, teams trained in such exotic locales as Evansville and French Lick, Ind., where the Chicago Cubs and Chicago White Sox, respectively, trained in 1943 and 1944. The East Coast teams didn't stray too far from home, either: The Brooklyn Dodgers trained at the West Point Field House between drills, and the Boston Braves trained at Choate School in Wallingford, Connecticut.

When the war ended, normalcy resumed—and that included baseball, which returned to springs spent mostly in Florida and Arizona. As travel and demographics changed, so did spring training. Rather than writing off spring training as a necessary expense, baseball teams saw spring training evolve into a profit center. Rather than being limited to boozy journalists and clubby insiders, spring training became open to everyone with enough money for admission.

And the reason for spring training changed as well, from a team-building exercise to a month-long advertisement for the regular season. Today very few roster spots are decided in spring training, and in this era of multimillion contracts players are working out in the winter, coming into camp already in shape. Major-league teams really don't need six weeks to determine rosters, but spring training is such a great advertisement for baseball that it would be impossible to scale back.

Photo: Scottsdale Charros in the 1950s. The Charros still are an important part of spring training at Scottsdale Stadium.

ARIZONA AND THE CACTUS LEAGUE

With a concentration of ten training complexes and 15 teams providing entertainment every day in March, Cactus League games have emerged in recent years as one of the great sports experiences on earth.

The Cactus League record for attendance was set in 2017, when 1.94 million spectators attended games in the greater Phoenix area and Las Vegas. That broke the previous total attendance of 1.902 million, set in 2016. Numbers have been

lower since, thanks to fewer scheduled games and the cance-
lation of a portion of the schedule thanks to the COVID-19
pandemic. Still, there's no doubt spring baseball is a major
tourism draw.

When Arizona interests lured the Giants and the Indians
for spring training in 1947, spring training was a different
beast in terms of economics and schedules. Teams had trained
out West many times before World War II—most notably the
Chicago Cubs, who first trained in Santa Monica in 1905 and
then on California's Catalina Island between 1922 and 1942—
and the economics were simple. Owners would get some
small community to subsidize spring training with direct
payments and cheap or free lodging. Teams would spend a
few weeks training (or drying out, in some cases), and then
those ballclubs would hit the road, barnstorming their way
home.

But as baseball became a big business, so did spring training. Owners were working every angle in search of more
revenue, and spring training became one obvious target. With
players basically working for free (salaries didn't kick in until
the season started), spring training was a way to generate
revenue without a lot of overhead.

In fact, the early history of spring training in Arizona
involves barnstorming teams. The Chicago White Sox barn-
stormed in 1909 before the season start, stopping in Yuma for
a match against a local team. Both the Cubs and White Sox
made stops in Arizona during spring training for the next
thirty-some years, and in 1929 the Detroit Tigers became the
first team to train in Arizona, setting up residence at Riverside Park in Phoenix. Staying true to form, the Tigers played a
whopping two games there before barnstorming their way
back to Detroit.

Barnstorming gradually gave way to longer stints at
training camp; instead of traveling and playing where the

fans lived, baseball teams coaxed fans to come to them. Baseball, sun, cheap beer, and access to stars: the formula was clear.

The roots of the Cactus League became a reality in 1947, when Horace Stoneham's New York Giants and Bill Veeck's Cleveland Indians took up residence in Phoenix and Tucson, respectively. That Veeck ended up in Tucson wasn't a surprise —he loved the Southwest and at the time owned a ranch near Tucson. Stoneham was a natural for Phoenix, as he was developing business interests in the area. Stoneham went one step even further than Veeck, constructing a luxury development in conjunction with spring training, a route that several team owners took over the years (and are still taking; more than one owner has floated the idea of combining a spring ballpark with a big-buck development). The Indians' home was known as Randolph Baseball Park when the Indians began training there; it was later renamed Hi Corbett Field and is now the home of the University of Arizona Wildcats baseball program.

INSIDER'S TIP
There's a bit of romantic history surrounding the decision by Stoneham to locate Giants spring training in Phoenix: that he was so taken by the Buckhorn Baths in East Mesa that he decided to bring the team west instead of returning to Miami, where the team trained in 1946. At least, that's the line from former Buckhorn Baths owner Alice Sliger, one that's repeated time and time again in the media.

It makes for a great story, and there's some truth to it. But Horace Stoneham also made money via real-estate investments, and he wasn't shy about using his baseball teams in association with his properties. In

Arizona, Stoneham ended up developing a resort in Casa Grande after looking at other investments in the area. (He wasn't the only developer to use a team as a lure; the New York Yankees trained in Arizona to further the development efforts of team owner Del Webb, who created the original Sun City in the Phoenix area.) Stoneham also did the same thing in Minnesota as owner of the Minneapolis Millers, buying large parcels of suburban land for a potential ballpark site when he was looking to move the Giants there.

Still, there was certainly a real allure to the Buckhorn Baths, and a mineral bath there was a tradition for players training in the area. Leo Durocher was a devotee, as were Ernie Banks and Willie Mays. The mineral baths may not have been the major reason why Stoneham scheduled spring training in Phoenix, but it ended up being a major reason why the team returned —although, in fact, the team trained in Florida in 1951.

The Cactus League was born in 1954 when the Baltimore Orioles signed to train in Yuma, joining the Indians, Cubs, and Giants in the state. Teams would come and go—the Red Sox replaced the Orioles in 1959, for instance—but more and more teams were attracted to Arizona after Veeck and Stoneham's arrival.

The Giants were replaced by the New York Yankees in 1951, under a unique one-year switch for the two franchises. Yankees co-owner Del Webb had extensive business dealings in Arizona, both as a developer (Pueblo Gardens in Tucson) and as a contractor (Hughes Missile Plant in Tucson), and he was eying other development opportunities in the state. (He would later launch Sun City, the groundbreaking senior community in the Phoenix suburbs, opening with five model homes on January 1, 1960.) What better way to promote the Del Webb Corporation than a Yankees spring tenure in Phoenix?

The expansion Los Angeles Angels played some games in Arizona in 1961 despite training in Palm Springs, California, while the expansion Houston Colt .45s played at Geronimo Park in Apache Junction. Most were lured with economic incentives: communities were all too willing to build facilities for teams, who benefited from a growing fan base (i.e.: transplanted retirees) and a growing economy. Some decisions, however, were more accidental. When the Seattle Pilots moved to Milwaukee in 1970, owner Bud Selig decided to keep the team's training base in Arizona, since he wintered in Scottsdale.

After the Cubs and Red Sox departed in 1966, the Cactus League was down to a troubling four teams, with two of those—the Angels and Cubs—training in California. (Over the years, teams continued to shift between Arizona and Florida: the Indians, Rangers, Royals, Red Sox, and Orioles have trained in both states.)

Changes in the 1969 spring training season saved the league. The Oakland Athletics moved to Mesa's Rendezvous Park after team owner Charlie O. Finley flirted with cities like Chandler in previous years, the expansion San Diego Padres began training at Yuma's Desert Sun Stadium, and the Seattle Pilots set up spring operations in Tempe Diablo Stadium.

By 1977, there were eight teams training in Arizona.

Baseball's move toward the West also hastened the growth of the Cactus League: with the Los Angeles Dodgers' relocation to a Glendale training facility, all eight Western MLB teams trained in Arizona. If you're running the Seattle Mariners or the San Diego Padres, an Arizona locale makes it far easier for fans and the media to attend spring training.

Today, the Cactus League is a lively institution in Phoenix. The 2010 arrival of the Cincinnati Reds gave Arizona 15 teams, the most in the Cactus League's history. We've seen new and renovated facilities emerge the last several years, as demand for baseball still continues to grow. For baseball fans, it's an abundance of riches, as you're never too far from a practice or a game no matter where you are in the Valley of the Sun.

TOURING PHOENIX AND SCOTTSDALE

With 15 teams training in the region, the Valley of the Sun hosts the entire Cactus League, combining the spirit of the Wild West with a bustling economy and a diverse population to create one of the largest metropolitan areas in the country. The total population in the region, per the last Census, now exceeds 5 million, with 1.651 million in Phoenix city limits, a half-million residents in Mesa and a quarter-million residents in Scottsdale and Glendale.

Understanding diversity (and we don't mean that in a politically correct way) is the key to understanding the greater Phoenix area. Spend any time in the area and you realize that there's no "one" Phoenix; instead, Phoenix is made up of interconnected communities, and part of the fun is exploring its many facets. And while we refer to Phoenix, we're really referring to the general area. Only one team, the Milwaukee Brewers, trains in Phoenix proper; the rest train in the suburbs.

Greater Phoenix is made up of the following areas:

- Downtown Phoenix is the city's sports and entertainment center. It's not the sort of high-traffic, concentrated commercial area you find in cities like San Francisco or Denver, but rather a laid-back collection of neighborhoods: some artsy, some commercial, some touristy, and some sports-oriented. We are assuming that you will be the most interested in sports-centric offerings in downtown Phoenix. Normally Chase Field, the home of the Arizona Diamondbacks, is empty until the end of spring training, when the Diamondbacks schedule a few exhibition games to put the ballpark through its paces. Those who seek to combine other sports during a visit will want to hit a Phoenix Suns game at Footprint Center, located next to Chase Field. In addition, baseball fans tend to hang around downtown sports bars like Majerle's (which we'll discuss later) after an afternoon game.
- The Camelback Corridor is a repository of serious money in the Valley. Many corporations call this

area home, while much of the high-end shopping in the region can be found there as well.

- Scottsdale is the upscale part of town, but downtown Scottsdale is also home to an area celebrating the Wild West and Phoenix's place in the white settlement of the West. (We'll also discuss Scottsdale in more detail in the San Francisco Giants chapter.)
- Tempe is home to Arizona State University, considered one of the best party colleges in the country. The action—both with bars and restaurants—takes place along or near Mill Avenue in Tempe. (We'll discuss Tempe in more depth in the Los Angeles Angels and Chicago Cubs chapters.)
- Mesa is largely a residential area to the east of Tempe. (We'll discuss Mesa in more depth in The Athletics chapter.)
- The northwestern and western suburbs have evolved into their own little spring-training worlds, with seven teams training in four facilities. Surprise, Goodyear, Glendale, and Peoria have grown and evolved with their own distinct identities. It's taken a while for these areas to develop, to be sure, but today a game on the west side of the Valley can be the centerpiece of a really great day.

NAVIGATING THE VALLEY OF THE SUN

Despite its size, the Valley of the Sun is surprisingly easy to navigate. Once you master your location relative to the freeways or to one of the major streets in the region, you stand a much better chance of not getting lost in a new area.

Why? Because the entire Valley is built in a grid system extending to the outer regions of the area. Freeways and bypasses intersect the grid at convenient points, making Phoenix and the surrounding area easy and convenient to navigate.

Two major freeways service the area: I-10 and I-17. I-10 enters the region from the west, where it's known as the Papago Freeway, running through the center of Phoenix and then heading south to Tempe and Tucson. This is the one freeway you'll spend some time driving, as it's the best way to reach the western and northwestern suburbs. I-17 (Black Canyon Freeway) comes in from the north and loops south of downtown before merging with I-10 (the merged stretch is called the Maricopa Freeway) near Sky Harbor International Airport.

Highway 60 (Grand Avenue) runs through the northwest quadrant of the region from downtown Phoenix all the way past Surprise. When you look at maps, you'll be tempted to take Highway 60 from the center of town to Peoria and Surprise. Don't. Highway 60 is filled with stop lights and traffic and is rarely worth the fuss. Instead, use Highway 101 as a shortcut. Highway 101 loops around the north side of town and is a true freeway. To get to Peoria from downtown, the quickest way is not the most direct way—Highway 60—but rather taking Highway 10 to Highway 101 and then heading north. Highway 101 is also the fastest way to reach the Maryvale neighborhood, Peoria, and Surprise.

INSIDER'S TIP

If you drive during spring training, an app like Apple Maps or Google Maps will be your friend. We find there is plenty of congestion on Phoenix freeways all day, and it's nice to have an app that can route you around some of this congestion.

INSIDER'S TIP
You won't see Maryvale on a map of the region. Technically, Maryvale is a Phoenix neighborhood, located in the southwestern part of Phoenix. The Milwaukee Brewers are the only team to train within Phoenix city limits. Every other team trains in the suburbs.

Once in the city, there are some major streets that will get you anywhere: Washington Street, Buckeye Road, Van Buren Street, McDowell Road, Thomas Road, Indian School Road, and Camelback Road are all major east-west streets that will usually get you close to where you want to go. Again, a navigation app like Apple Maps or Google Maps will be your friend; often one of these major city streets will be a faster route than a freeway, and a good app will route you there.

INSIDER'S TIP
You can easily figure out the approximate location of an address. All addresses begin at Central Avenue (which runs north-south through downtown) and Washington Street (which runs east-west through downtown). Streets are on the east side of town, while avenues are on the west side of town. Camelback Road is 50 blocks north of Washington Street, so you can usually determine where you are relative to Camelback and Washington.

ARRIVING IN PHOENIX

Sky Harbor International Airport is the major airport in the region, centrally located to most spring-training venues, and most of you will fly in and out of it. In the past, Sky Harbor International Airport presented a challenging experience, with multiple terminals and a confusing layout. Flying in and out of Sky Harbor International Airport is now a much more pleasant experience, thanks to a multiyear renovation and modernization, as has the addition of a PHX Sky Train that runs between all three terminals and a station at 44th Street and Washington Avenue. That station is also a connecting point for the Valley Metro Rail system. If your last flight in and out of Phoenix came years ago and you remember bottlenecks at the security checks and long lines at the limited number of food and drink vendors, you will be pleasantly surprised by the wide concourses, the abundance of open lines at security, and the more robust selection of food and drink vendors.

Alas, Valley Metro Rail probably won't be a factor for you. Light rail has certainly changed Phoenix, but it's not really impacted spring-training venues. In fact, no spring venue is served by light rail. However, you can plan a trip around light rail and ridesharing, as many hotels are close to the light-rail line. Once at your hotel, you can then use Uber or Lyft to get to the training complex.

That will require a bit of planning. Our advice: you will want to rent a car unless you plan on spending all your time directly next to a ballpark or dealing with ridesharing logistics. We'll say it again: Phoenix sprawls, and no one walks. Public transit is good if you want to get around the center city and downtown Scottsdale, but is completely lacking for those making their way to spring-training facilities. To make your way around in Phoenix, a car is essential; parking in most popular areas frequented by spring-training fans is almost always free and plentiful.

Speaking of car rentals: there is no car rental at Sky Harbor International Airport. The rental agencies are located at an offsite Rental Car Center. No bus anymore, though: the PHX Sky Train runs from Terminals 3 and 4 to the Rental Car Center. It takes between six and eight minutes to travel from the Rental Car Center to the two Sky Harbor International Airport terminals.

Many fans can fly directly to Sky Harbor, instead of going through the hassle of connecting flights and what seems to be inevitable delays. In each chapter we discuss the status of flights in and out of Sky Harbor from specific cities. Every major airline serves Sky Harbor, including Air Canada, American, Alaska, Allegiant, British Airways, Delta, Frontier, JetBlue, Southwest, Spirit, Sun Country, United, and WestJet.

*Sky Harbor International Airport, 3400 E. Sky Harbor Blvd., Phoenix; 602/273-3300; **skyharbor.com**.*

INSIDER'S TIP

Even though the Valley sprawls, the spring-training sites are conveniently located in relationship to the airport. To reach Scottsdale from the airport, take Hwy. 202 (the Red Mountain Freeway) to Hwy. 101. To reach downtown Phoenix, take I-10 west. To reach Surprise or Peoria, take I-10 west to Hwy. 101 north. To reach Glendale or Goodyear, take I-10 west. To reach Tempe or Mesa, take I-10 or Hwy. 60 (the Superstition Freeway). We'd recommend using an app like Apple Maps to plot out driving routes.

A smaller airport, Phoenix-Mesa Gateway, features flights from Allegiant Airlines, which serves many midsized and smaller markets nationally—the likes of Billings, Bozeman, Omaha, the Quad Cities (Moline), Rockford, Spokane, South Bend, Houston, Fort Wayne, Bellingham, Cincinnati, and Las Vegas. In addition, Sun Country flies from Minneapolis-St. Paul. Rental-car firms Alamo, Avis, Hertz, and Enterprise operate in the terminal. Yes, the services are more limited at Phoenix-Mesa Gateway, but you'll get in and out of the airport quicker than at Sky Harbor, and if you're from the likes of Billings or the Quad Cities, you'll appreciate the convenience of a direct flight. *Phoenix-Mesa Gateway Airport, 6033 S. Sossaman Rd., Mesa;* **gatewayairport.com.**

PHOENIX ATTRACTIONS

With so many spring-training facilities in a concentrated area, you'll be able to hit at least one game daily during your stay, or two if teams have scheduled a night game or two. This is now easier than it once was. MLB teams have been scheduling more night games in recent years, while both Arizona State University and Grand Canyon University play many night games. You'll spend much of your time at the ballpark, but you will probably want a few more diversions during the course of your stay. There's something for everyone in Phoenix. We'll list some of the more popular indoor and outdoor attractions here. (The many attractions of Scottsdale are listed later in this chapter.) Here we'll pass along some family-friendly activities. The first three are located in east Phoenix and in close proximity to one another.

The Desert Botanical Garden is 50 acres of trails and exhibits covering the ecosystem of the Sonoran Desert. It's home to 139 endangered species of plants, as well as the most cacti you've seen in your life. *Desert Botanical Garden, 1201 N. Galvin Pkwy., Phoenix; 480/941-1225;* **dbg.org**. *Adults, $16.95; children (3-17), $16.95.*

Another great hiking spot: Papago Park. For those just wanting to get outside, there are some level trails through the desert brush, perfect for those of us who might not be in perfect shape after a long winter mostly spent indoors. (Remember: stay hydrated.) For those wanting a challenge, check out the rock-climbing trails. The location in the middle of the West Valley is convenient from all of Phoenix. *Papago*

Park, 625 N. Galvin Pkwy., Phoenix; 602/495-5458; **phoenix.-**
gov/parks/trails/locations/papago-park.

Located near both the Desert Botanical Garden and
Papago Park is the Phoenix Zoo, a great place to take the kids.
The layout is organized by theme—there are separate trails
with African, Tropics, and Arizona themes, along with a Children's Trail. There are over 1,300 animals on display, and
traversing the whole place should take about three hours.
Phoenix Zoo, 455 N. Galvin Pkwy., Phoenix; 602/273-1341;
phoenixzoo.org. *Adults, $39.95; children 3-12, $29.95; discounts*
for online presales.

Camelback Mountain, located in the northeast part of
town, is a popular destination for hikers and nature lovers.
There are four trails—two for inexperienced hikers, running
less than an eighth of a mile, and two for very experienced
hikers, reaching 1.5 miles. You can find parking for the
various trails at East McDonald Drive and Tatum Boulevard.
Some warning: even on the shorter trails you run some risk of
dehydration and sunburn, so bring water and sunscreen.

Architecture buffs will be fascinated by Taliesin West,
Frank Lloyd Wright's winter home, and the Biltmore, with a
design inspired by Wright's architecture style. Located in
eastern Scottsdale, Taliesin West takes its inspiration from the
Arizona landscape. Like all Wright buildings, the scale is intimate and low to the ground, while almost all of the materials
were locally sourced. *Taliesin West, 12621 Frank Lloyd Wright*
Blvd., Scottsdale; 480/860-2700; **franklloydwright.org.** *Prices*
vary depending on length of tour.

The Arizona Biltmore may be the most unique hotel in
Phoenix. Located in the Camelback Corridor, the Arizona
Biltmore was designed by Albert Chase McArthur, a former
student of Frank Lloyd Wright, who served as the consulting
architect. The Wright influence is obvious: the hotel is
constructed of precast concrete blocks (a building material

favored by Wright) in a geometric pattern, with the unique "Biltmore Blocks" designed by local artist Emry Kopta. Chewing-gum magnate William Wrigley Jr. was an early investor in the project, and by 1930 owned the entire place, but curiously he never combined it with his other great passion, the Chicago Cubs, who instead trained for many of the Wrigley years on California's Catalina Island at the original Wrigley Field. During the 1930s and 1940s, it was *the* place to winter in Phoenix; Irving Berlin wrote "White Christmas" while lounging poolside at the Biltmore, and Marlyn Monroe adored her time there. Stop by the outdoor Spire Bar and imagine Berlin humming tunes poolside, or The Wright Bar, where the Tequila Sunrise was invented, even if you're not staying there. The lobby is an oasis and a nice place for a post-game cocktail. Though Wright was not the architect of record and was a little churlish about not receiving what he deemed to be enough credit for the Arizona Biltmore design, his presence can be felt everywhere: subsequent renovations were overseen by Taliesin Associated Architects and decorative elements designed by Wright, including the Sprites of Midway Gardens in Chicago, were later installed. *Arizona Biltmore, 2400 E. Missouri Av., Phoenix; 855/689-2878; **arizonabiltmore.com**.*

Speaking of the Camelback Corridor: a pleasant evening can be spent at the nearby Biltmore Fashion Park. All the major trendy stores are represented in the open-air mall, but our preference is to do dinner at True Food Kitchen, Zinburger, Blanco Cocina, Breakfast Club, Capital Grille, Cheesecake Factory or Seasons 52, and then stroll the grounds. *Biltmore Fashion Park, 2400 E. Missouri Av., Phoenix; 602/955-6600; **shopbiltmore.com**.*

Speaking of William Wrigley Jr.: In the context of a spring-training guide, it's natural that our point of reference will be his beloved Cubs and, to a lesser degree, the Arizona Biltmore. One more local attraction worth your while if you want to know more about the innovative genius: The Wrigley Mansion. Once slated for demolition and then restored in 2021 by the late Geordie Hormel (yes, one of the Hormel heirs) and his wife Jamie, The Wrigley Mansion serves both as an illustration of Wrigley's passions and a fine-dining destination, with great views of the Valley. In 1932 Wrigley built the residence as a 50th-anniversary gift to his wife, Ada. Restored and expanded, its architecture includes elements of Spanish, California Monterey, and Mediterranean styles. As a homage to another Wrigley passion, original tiles still grace The Mansion, having been shipped from the Wrigley family's tile factory on Catalina Island and carted up the hill by donkey. Some of the private residence has been converted to private dining rooms, while multiple restaurant bars and restaurants occupy both new and old parts of the complex. We'd recommend a tour and dinner. *The Wrigley Mansion, 2501 E. Telawa Tr., Phoenix; 602/955-4079; **wrigleymansion.com**.*

The Heard Museum focuses on indigenous peoples of the Americas, with an emphasis on American Indian tribes and other cultures of the Southwest. In an era where the past is constantly being reevaluated and previously ignored forms like American Indian art are exposed to a wider audience, the Heard Museum is an essential experience for anyone wanting to know more about Phoenix and the U.S. Southwest. *The Heard Museum, 2301 N. Central Av., Phoenix; 602/252-8840; **heard.org**. Adults, $22.50; seniors, $18; students and children over 6, $9.*

Another museum of note—and one perfect for the kids—is the Musical Instrument Museum. With 6,500 objects on display and another 10,000 in the archives, plenty of extended descriptions, and live concerts, the Musical Instrument Museum is a surprisingly immersive experience. *Musical Instrument Museum, 4725 E. Mayo Blvd., Phoenix; 480/478-6000;*

mim.org. *Adults, $20; teens (13-19), $15; child (4-12), $10; children (3 & under), free.*

These is much more to the greater Phoenix area than just these highlights. We go into depth on the areas surrounding the ballparks in the following chapters.

RECOMMENDED PHOENIX RESTAURANTS

There is an amazing diversity of restaurants in the Valley of the Sun. The region helped make Southwestern cuisine one of the most innovative food movements of the last 35 years, and today you can find world-class restaurants throughout the region. You can also find a wide range of sports bars and restaurants, too, if your tastes don't run to haute cuisine. In this section, we'll give you a little of each. We also will list recommended restaurants close to each of the spring-training ballparks. We are also concentrating on the center of Phoenix, as we'll list sports-centric restaurants and bars near all the training complexes as well.

Majerle's Sports Grill, located in downtown Phoenix, is one of the traditional sports bars in town. Dan Majerle ("Marley") was a popular forward for the Phoenix Suns, and when Footprint Center was completed in 1992, the 3-point sharpshooter went into the sports-bar business and opened up Majerle's in the oldest commercial building in downtown Phoenix. *Majerle's Sports Grill, 24 N. 2nd St., Phoenix; 602/253-0118; **majerles.com.***

If you find yourself in the vicinity of Chase Field at night after a few cocktails, drop by Lo-Lo's Chicken and Waffles. Phoenix isn't known for its soul food, but Lo-Lo's is in a class by itself when it comes to that magic combination of chicken and waffles—a much better pairing than you'd think. *Lo-Lo's Chicken and Waffles, 1220 S. Central Av., Phoenix; 602/340-1304; **loloschickenandwaffles.com**.* Also popular: the Scottsdale location, conveniently located near Scottsdale Stadium. *3133 N. Scottsdale Rd., Scottsdale; 480/945-1920.*

For Mexican seafood, check out Mariscos Playa Hermosa. We think of Mexican cuisine as a monolithic entity, but regional flavors are important south of the border. In the case of Mariscos Playa Hermosa, the cuisine is not only Mexican but the restaurant specializes in the seafood cuisine found in Hermosillo. You normally don't think of great seafood when you think of landlocked Phoenix, but Mariscos Playa Hermosa shatters that stereotype. *Mariscos Playa Hermosa, 1605 E. Garfield St., Phoenix; 602/462-1563;* ***mariscosplayahermosa.com.***

Phoenix has more than its share of steakhouses, and one of the more notable ones is Rustlers Rooste. Whether or not you buy into the mythology of the place—that the restaurant was formerly a hideaway for cattle rustlers—there's no doubt that the Rooste provides an impressive view of the Valley. *Rustler's Rooste, 8383 S. 48th St., Phoenix; 602/431-6474;* ***rustlersrooste.com.***

There's no better example of truth in advertising than the Cold Beer & Cheeseburgers (***coldbeers.com***) chain in the Valley, where the emphasis is on—what else?—cold beer and cheeseburgers. But the menu features more than just those staples, including sandwiches, cocktails, and salads, and the many locations—Phoenix, Scottsdale, Tempe, Surprise, etc.— are great sports bars as well. There's also a location in Chase Field, with a porch and awning overlooking the playing field.

This doesn't even scrape the surface of good restaurants in Phoenix. These are some opening suggestions, but you don't ever have to go very far throughout the entire region to find some good food, whether it be tacos sold out of a modest truck or four-star chef-driven high cuisine. Phoenix is an interesting mix of high-end restaurants and low-rent dive bars, so you're never really far away from a great meal or a cheap drink.

Or a great drink. One trend we've noted with huge approval is the emergence of elegant, adventurous cocktail bars. One notable effort encompasses three cocktail bars sporting a turn-of-the-century environment at Century Grand in Phoenix's Arcadia neighborhood. Century Grand features different immersive experiences. Our favorite: Platform 18, a 90-minute trip aboard a recreation of a high-end Presidential Pullman car, with the windows displaying a train trip through the Rocky Mountains. The other experience worth noting: drinks served at a Grey Hen Rx apothecary, complete with New Orleans-inspired cocktails. We've done the Platform 18 experience and can recommend it: reservations are required, no food available, and you're limited to a 90-minute journey. *Century Grand, 3626 E. Indian School Rd., Phoenix; 602/844-4643; centurygrandphx.com.*

Another trend we've seen in Phoenix over the last three or four years: the rise of small, neighborhood joints. Usually featuring limited hours with different offerings, these modest restaurants and breweries are made for a relaxed experience. While the offerings at a sports and entertainment district are big and loud and a volume business, these neighborhood hangouts are laid back. An example of a neighborhood joint worth a drive is Nogales Hot Dogs, operating in several Phoenix locations. All are basically food stands with open seating under a tent. The specialty of the house: a great take on a Sonoran hot dog, a Phoenix delicacy. The $5.50 Sonoran Hot Dog involves a bacon-wrapped frank topped with pinto beans, tomatoes, cheese, onions, and mayo, with additional toppings like guacamole available at a condiment bar, served on a Mexican-style bun. If you're in the area, we'd recommend it, but you should also always be aware that you're never too far away from a similar laid back hangout in much of Phoenix.

INSIDER'S TIP

Remember that all the spring-training facilities in Phoenix are fairly close together. It's easy to move around the city, so don't assume that just because an attraction or restaurant is in Scottsdale or Tempe you should avoid it. Tempe, Scottsdale, Mesa, and Phoenix are all adjoining communities, as are Peoria, Goodyear, and Surprise. We list hotels and restaurants by locale, but don't let these boundaries stop you from perusing the chapters for all the ballparks in search of a restaurant or attraction: you're never really far away from anything in the Valley of the Sun.

THE WEST VALLEY: STILL SHINY AND NEW

When Peoria Stadium opened in 1994, it was out in the middle of nowhere. City officials sought spring training as a way to spur development, an attraction that would bring in residents, businesses, and tourists.

Today, some 30 years after Peoria Stadium opened, the promise of suburban development is finally fulfilled. For many years, the area around the ballpark was filled with skeevy chain restaurants, dead during most of the year. Today, the Peoria market is hot, and the P83 Entertainment District is a success. You can expect plenty of traffic and crowded restaurants during the spring-training season as locals and fans descend on bars, restaurants, movie theaters, and retail. We've grown to love spending time at places like The Moon Saloon. We'll have a lot more on the P83 Entertainment District in our Peoria Stadium chapter.

Similarly popular is the Westgate Entertainment District, anchored by Desert Diamond Arena and located next to State Farm Stadium. The Westgate Entertainment District generates a lot of traffic at any time, between a host of restaurants and bars combined with live music and a 20-screen AMC movie theater-complex. We'll cover the Westgate Entertainment District in more depth in our Camelback Ranch–Glendale chapter.

As you probably have figured out, entertainment districts are big in Phoenix. Communities like Glendale, Peoria, Mesa, and Tempe have invested plenty in the establishment of these districts, designed to entertain the locals and attract the tourists. Not every effort has been successful (a proposed entertainment district next to Goodyear Ballpark is still in the works), but they've proven to be an established amenity in the West Valley.

SCOTTSDALE: UPSCALE MEETS KITSCH

Downtown Scottsdale is a curious mix of the kitsch and the artsy; it's where the well-heeled in the region step out to buy a cowboy T-shirt for the grandkids and then dine at an upscale restaurant before hitting the well-regarded Scottsdale Art Museum.

Of course, another way to put it is that Scottsdale has something for everyone, ranging from a slew of touristy Old West shops in Old Town to the upscale department stores at the Scottsdale Fashion Mall. This means you can easily entertain yourself for days in Scottsdale between spring-training games in the Valley.

There are four major districts to downtown Scottsdale: Fifth Avenue, Main Street, Old Town, and Marshall Way. Fifth Avenue features upscale shopping and dining; the Marshall Way Arts District features art galleries specializing in contemporary art from local artists, as well as a wide variety of regionally produced jewelry; Main Street is one of the largest concentrations of art galleries in the world; and Old Town features the aforementioned Wild West kitsch. Also worth noting: the Civic Center Mall area, which combines public amenities like the Civic Center Library and the Scottsdale Center for the Performing Arts with plenty of bars, restaurants, and hotels.

The San Francisco Giants play at Scottsdale Stadium, close to Old Town and the Arts District, which we'll cover in its own chapter.

TODAY'S SCOTTSDALE BASEBALL HOTSPOTS

Scottsdale has traditionally been the center of spring training in the Valley of the Sun. While that's not necessarily true anymore, it's certainly home to the most restaurants catering to spring-training fans and baseball nostalgia. Here are some traditional choices.

Bob and Mary Brower catered to baseball fans and players at the Coach House in Scottsdale. Of course, this was back in the 1960s and the Boston Red Sox was the team training in Scottsdale. But some things remain the same: The Brower family still owns the Coach House, and it's still a spring-training hangout. The Coach House opened in 1959, located in an old house but expanded since: the large Coach House Tavern sign is the original. It's not uncommon to see a player or three relaxing with an adult beverage on the patio of Scottsdale's oldest tavern. It opens at 6 a.m. for that morning snort and closes at 1 a.m. for that post-game celebration. No, this isn't the place to order a designer cocktail; it's a place to order a shot with a beer chaser. Recommended if you want to step back to the 1960s. *Coach House Tavern, 7011 E. Indian School Rd., Scottsdale; 480/990-3433;* **coachhousescottsdale.com.**

More a hangout for sportswriters than for players or coaches (yes, there are still writers with boots on the ground in spring training, as opposed to bloggers opining from their desk next to the basement water heater), Karsen's Grill is another traditional Old Town spring-training hangout. Like any good hangout for sportswriters, Karsen's Grill is basically a dive bar with good deep-fried foods (pickles!), a wicked social-media presence, and a friendly owner. Highly recommended. *Karsen's Grill, 7246 East 1st St. #101, Scottsdale; 480/990-7660; karsensgrill.net.*

Billed as the successor to shuttered spring-training landmarks, Frasher's Tavern is less than a mile from Scottsdale Stadium and is geared toward spring-training fans, complete with plenty of baseball memorabilia, a classic interior with plenty of wood paneling, and a menu heavy on steaks and seafood—and the inevitable toasted ravioli, as proprietor George Frasher grew up a Cardinals fan in St. Louis. *Frasher's Tavern, 4180 N. Drinkwater Blvd., Scottsdale; 480/429-9545; frasherstavern.com.*

GHOSTS OF SPRING TRAININGS PAST

For many insiders, it wasn't really a trip to spring training without a stop at one of the classic spring-training hangouts of Scottsdale. Alas, most are gone.

Not long ago patrons came in for one last dinner at Don & Charlie's, located on the edge of downtown Scottsdale. It was the ultimate baseball insider hangout, frequented by general managers, scouts, and broadcasters: Bob Uecker, for example, was a regular.

But the restaurant closed, and a plan to open a new Don & Charlie's in a boutique hotel on the site cratered. The new hotel—Senna House—is there, but no new Don & Charlie's. Giants and Brewers officials may come and go, but Don

Larson was a constant in spring training, whether it be chatting with patrons at his sports bar or serving up press-box meals at Scottsdale Stadium.

Also gone: The Italian Grotto in Old Town Scottsdale. A traditional player haunt, The Grotto was a sports bar cum traditional Italian restaurant, with lots of pasta on the menus and lots of sports memorabilia on the walls. There is another Italian restaurant in the space: La Locanda Italian Bistro (*6830 E. 5th Av., Suite 108, Scottsdale; 480/284-6511;* **lalocandaaz.com**), offering a more upscale dining experience at the traditional red-sauce Italian Grotto and without the emphasis on sports.

Another Cactus League institution whose ghosts still haunts downtown Scottsdale: the Pink Pony, located on Scottsdale Road near Scottsdale Stadium. You can't miss the place: the ghost of the Pink Pony sign is still present, as the bar/restaurant space has been unoccupied for several years. Opening in 1952, the Pink Pony was where Los Angeles Angels owner Gene Autry held court at the same Naugahyde booth every spring, where Giants players and coaches enjoyed a postgame meal, where players like Ted Williams and Mickey Mantle dined while training in Arizona, and where scouts gathered to discuss prospects. Long before Don & Charlie's, the Pink Pony was the place for MLB insiders to hang out during spring training, as well as a destination for celebrities: Robert Wagner and Natalie Wood had their post-wedding dinner there after getting married at the nearby Hotel Valley Ho. In recent years it had been renovated under new ownership (after a few closures), removing the old-timey look in favor of modern mid-century décor. Alas, the place was stripped after the latest iteration failed, and while the location is prime, there's no replacement yet. Sadly, a visit there during August 2023 revealed nothing but faded PINK PONY shadows on the front facade, a sad reminder of what was a spring-training hotspot for decades. Given how hip retro is, it's amazing the space has been unoccupied for so long. It's money, baby.

SCOTTSDALE DINING AND DRINKING

Apart from the traditional choices, downtown Scottsdale features a wide range of dining and drinking options in all sorts of genres and price ranges. Though this is a fairly extensive list of restaurants and hotspots, it's by no means complete. We cover additional Scottsdale hotspots in our Giants chapter.

Our favorite spot before a Giants home game at Scottsdale Stadium is the Sugar Bowl Ice Cream Parlor. The specialty, as you might expect, is ice cream (try the Top Hat sundae or a Dutch Chocolate malt), but the throwback menu also features tasty sandwiches and burgers. It's the most kid-friendly place in downtown Scottsdale—and that extends to Giants minor-leaguers as well, as they'll occasionally show up for a treat after practice. And yes, plenty of adults hit the place for some comfort food without kids in tow. Expect to wait for a table at lunch or dinner, and a line for an ice cream cone in the evening. *Sugar Bowl Ice Cream Parlor, 4005 N. Scottsdale Rd., Scottsdale; 480/946-0051;* **sugarbowlscottsdale.com.**

Close to the ballpark: RnR Gastropub, jammed with Giants fans before and after games, especially during March Madness. The two-story dining patio makes for some great people watching, while most tables also have a view of big screens with basketball action. We'd recommend a reservation if you plan on weekend brunch before an afternoon game. *RnR Gastropub, 3737 N. Scottsdale Rd. Scottsdale; 480-945-3353;* **rnrscottsdale.com.**

Though there are several Zipps sports bars in Scottsdale, Tempe, and Phoenix, our favorite is Zipps Sports Grill Camelback, in the middle of Old Town Scottsdale. It's a great place to follow March Madness, as the outdoor deck features TVs and a firepit, perfect for viewing those evening basketball games. *Zipps Sports Grill Camelback, 7551 E. Camelback Rd., Scottsdale; 480/970-9507; zippssportsgrills.com.*

Citizen Public House is an upscale gastropub a longish walk from Scottsdale Stadium. It's more on the upscale side of the equation, with an above-average drink lineup and an eclectic food lineup that includes a great buttermilk fried chicken, the inevitable flat-iron steak, and more. Management has worked hard to attract Giants fans, and the effort has paid off. *Citizen Public House, 7111 E. 5th Av., Scottsdale; 480/398-4208; citizenpublichouse.com.*

Another upscale restaurant in Old Town worth a visit: FnB, a gastropub with an emphasis on farm-to-table cuisine, complete with an Arizona-only wine program. *FnB, 7125 E. 5th Av., #31, Scottsdale; 480-284-4777; fnbrestaurant.com.*

Nearby: Second Story Restaurant & Liquor Bar. Cocktails and high-end liquors are the specialty of the house. If the whole adobe/Southwestern thing is proving to be too much for you, Second Story's clubby atmosphere is a welcome change of pace. *Second Story, 4166 N. Scottsdale Rd., Suite 102, Scottsdale; 480/945-5555; secondstoryaz.com.*

Live music and cheap beer are featured at Old Town Tavern on the Civic Center Mall, where bands are scheduled every day the Giants are playing at Scottsdale Stadium. It's a small space and within a short walk of Scottsdale Stadium, so get there early for an outdoor table and cheap cocktails. *7320 E. Scottsdale Rd. Scottsdale; 480/945-2882; oldtowntavernaz.com.*

Also known for cheap drinks and a dive-bar atmosphere: The Rusty Spur Saloon, which features strong drinks, no beer on tap, and very limited seating. Still, the bar stools alone are worth a visit. The building has an interesting history. It originally was the Farmer's State Bank of Scottsdale when the building opened in 1921, but the bank didn't last long, closing during the Great Depression. Today it's one of Scottsdale's oldest bars, opening in 1951. Yes, there will be a band playing at lunchtime for those whose definition of Happy Hour begins in the a.m.; no, no one will shame the day drinkers; and yes, there will be a crowd beginning at the 10 a.m. opening. *The Rusty Spur Saloon, 7245 E. Main St., Scottsdale; 480/425-7787;* **rustyspursaloon.com**.

One more downtown sports bar to note: Social Tap, which features plenty of flat-screen TVs, an abundance of sports programming, a chill atmosphere, and some elevated bar food. *Social Tap, 4312 N. Brown Av., Scottsdale; 602/432-6719;* **socialtapscottsdaleaz.com**.

It's become a local chain of sorts in the South and Southwest, but the Scottsdale location of Culinary Dropout is our favorite, both for the decor and for the fried chicken and fondue. Yes, fondue. *Culinary Dropout, 7135 E. Camelback Rd., Suite 125, Scottsdale; 480/970-1700;* **culinarydropout.com**.

Old Town Tortilla Factory is located in a 75-year-old former adobe home in the heart of Old Town Scottsdale and features a 1,200-square-foot deck. The margaritas served here have won national acclaim, and it's hard to imagine anything better than sipping an excellent margarita under a clear desert sky at night. Honestly, it doesn't get any more Scottsdale than a laid-back dinner and drinks to end the day. *Old Town Tortilla Factory, 6910 E. Main St.; 480/945-4567;* **oldtowntortillafactory.com**.

Order yourself a sleek, modern drink like an Aperol Spritz or an Aged Old Fashioned at AZ 88 and hang out with the sleek and sexy of Scottsdale on the gorgeous patio. North of the Scottsdale Museum of Contemporary Art on the Civic Center Mall, AZ 88 is the embodiment of Scottsdale chic. It is also a place to do some serious drinking before or after a

Giants home game. *AZ 88, 7353 Scottsdale Mall, Scottsdale; 480/994-5576; az88.com.*

Grimaldi's Coal Brick-Oven Pizzeria is definitely an oddity or a pleasant surprise, depending on your point of view. We're not exactly sure how one of the best pizzerias in Brooklyn ended up with a Scottsdale outpost—never mind 11 across Arizona—but we're too busy scarfing down the thin-crust pizza to care. For those who don't worship the perfect pizza, there are calzones on the menu as well. *Grimaldi's Coal Brick-Oven Pizzeria, 4000 N. Scottsdale Rd., Scottsdale; 480/994-1100; grimaldispizzeria.com.*

One final outpost to note. Most of us come to spring training to indulge, and there's nothing more indulgent than a full bar with a wide selection of cigars. If this sounds like heaven to you, the Fox Cigar Bar is your place. With 34 flat screens broadcasting all manner of sports, a three-page-long selection of whiskies/bourbons/liquors, plenty of comfy chairs, and a huge walk-in humidor, the Fox Cigar Bar is the place for post-game relaxation. As a bonus, it's open until 2 a.m. *Fox Cigar Bar, 7443 E. 6th Av., Scottsdale; 480/214-5011; foxcigar.com.*

OLD TOWN SCOTTSDALE

Scottsdale is not a very old community. It began life as a housing development in 1894 when an Eastern banker named Albert Utley divided 40 acres of desert land into lots. The name Scottsdale comes from U.S. Chaplain Winfield Scott, whose promotional efforts attracted many of the earlier settlers.

Most of today's Old Town in downtown Scottsdale dates back to the 1920s or earlier, when the area experienced its first growth spurt. There are several remnants of the original Scottsdale in the Old Town area:

- Cavalliere Blacksmith Shop (*3805 N. Brown Av.; 480/945-6262*). George Cavalliere moved his family to Scottsdale in 1910 and opened a blacksmith shop on the edge of downtown Scottsdale. He originally set up shop in a metal building, which he replaced with the current adobe structure in 1920. The Cavalliere family still operates the blacksmith shop. Many of you will walk next to the Cavalliere Blacksmith shop when running between the Giants game and the downtown watering holes and not realize its link to the Scottsdale of old.
- The first post office in Scottsdale opened in 1928 and was a community gathering place when the mail was delivered from Phoenix. The building still stands and is now home to Porters Boot Corral (*3944 N. Brown Av.; 480/945-0868*).
- Our Lady of Perpetual Help Catholic Parish - Old Adobe Mission (*3821 N. Brown Av.; oldadobemission.org*) is a striking white building in Old Town. It dates back to 1933, when local Mexican residents volunteered their time and money to construct the church. The parish embarked on a restoration effort on the historic adobe building, and the result is a lovely building reminiscent of early Scottsdale.
- The Little Red Schoolhouse (*7333 E. Scottsdale Mall; 480/945-4499*), now home to the Scottsdale Historical Society (*scottsdalehistory.org*), was built in 1909 as a two-room schoolhouse. It housed the school through the 1960s and was then used for a variety of civic purposes.
- Los Olivos Mexican Patio (*7328 E. 2nd St.; 480/946-2256; losolivosrestaurants.com*), built in the 1950s,

originally housed a pool hall and a church before becoming a Mexican restaurant.

Not exactly an old original Scottsdale outpost, but Baseballism has a storefront in Old Town Scottsdale. There are plenty of unique T-shirts and caps here. You may have run across Baseballism at a popup; you may again in 2025. *Baseballism, 3961 N. Brown Av., Scottsdale; 480/947-2130;* ***baseballism.com.***

There's one other feature in Old Town worth checking out: the olive trees along Drinkwater Boulevard and Second Street. Winfield Scott, the founder of Scottsdale, planted them in 1896.

OTHER SPORTS IN THE AREA

In the event you have a spare moment during your spring trip to Phoenix, there are plenty of other sporting events to occupy your time.

Phoenix is a major-league city, with NBA games scheduled in February and March. The Phoenix Suns play at the downtown Footprint Center (formerly Talking Stick Resort Arena), one of the more intimate facilities in the NBA. With the Suns hiring coach Mike Budenholzer to make a run at an NBA Championship in 2025, the team is a hot draw, and the renovations to Footprint Center amp the energy level while turning the place into the world's largest sports bar. Buy your tickets early, as the Suns are a major draw no matter the team's record. The arena is next to Chase Field, with plenty of sports-related watering holes nearby. *Footprint Center, 201 E. Jefferson St., Phoenix; 602/379-7800;* ***footprintcenter.com.***

After a few years of play at a collegiate arena and failed attempts to land a site for a new arena, the NHL's Arizona Coyotes are no more, with the team moving to Salt Lake City for the 2024-2025 season and beyond. The Coyotes owners retained team marks and records, as well as rights to an expansion franchise should the team work out details for a new arena. For now, though, the Valley is down one major-league team.

Professional soccer came of age in Phoenix in 2017 with the emergence of Phoenix Rising in the United Soccer League (USL). USL Championship is a Division II league, second on the soccer pyramid to MLS. Phoenix Rising went from sparsely attended crowds at Peoria Stadium in 2016 to creating some serious buzz and attracting larger crowds at a modular stadium now in its third location, this time in Phoenix proper. The USL season slightly overlaps with spring training. The stadium here is strictly a pop-up affair, but well worth the trip. *Phoenix Rising FC Soccer Complex, 3801 East Washington Street; 623/594-9606; phxrisingfc.com.*

A free evening could entail a visit to see the Arizona State University Sun Devils playing at Phoenix Municipal Stadium, the former spring home of the Oakland Athletics, or a Grand Canyon University game in Phoenix. The ASU baseball program is traditionally strong and Phoenix Muni is always worth the trip, so we'll be covering the Sun Devils, Phoenix Muni, and GCU baseball in their own chapter.

FESTIVAL TIME!

The Innings Festival (*inningsfestival.com*), held at Tempe Beach Park in Tempe, was considered a success in 2024, with the likes of Red Hot Chili Peppers, Hozier, and Chris Stapleton headlining. It was designed for baseball fans: besides the headlining bands, the festival also featured appearances from retired players, baseball-themed games, and spring-training food. No word yet on a 2025 return.

Organizers say the M3F Music Festival (*m3ffest.com*) will

return in 2025. Held at Steele Indian School Park (300 E. Indian School Rd.) in Phoenix, M3F is a charity event with a very eclectic lineup.

Closing spring training 2024: Surprise's Out of the Park Music Fest (*outoftheparkmusicfest.com*), with the city promising a 2025 return. Held the last weekend of spring training, the Surprise Stadium event featured an eclectic musical lineup, food trucks galore, and plenty of beer on tap.

GOLF: A PRIME PURSUIT

A big reason why folks retire to Arizona: golf. The Valley of the Sun sports an abundance of golf courses, ranging from high-end private courses at the core of a planned development to notable municipal courses. Unless you have a good friend who lives on one of the high-end private courses, you'll need to go the public route—which can be most enjoyable. We cover some local courses in each chapter, but here are some courses worth the drive and near more than one spring-training facility.

Scottsdale's Troon North is regarded by golf insiders as one of the best public courses in the United States, which makes it worth the drive from anywhere in the Valley. Featuring two 18-hole Pinnacle and Monument courses designed by Tom Weiskopf and Jay Morrish, each at par 72, Troon North is designed to invoke British Open layouts. But it's uniquely an Arizona course, located in the shadows of Pinnacle Peak and following the landscape of Arizona's Sonoran Desert. They both play at slightly more than 7,000 yards, and they've been revamped in recent years by Weiskopf. Easily reached from Scottsdale Stadium and Salt River Fields at Talking Stick. *Troon North Golf Club, 10320 E. Dynamite Blvd., Scottsdale; 480/585-7700; troonnorthgolf.com.*

An affordable course in the middle of town is Grand

Canyon University Golf Course, the former Maryvale Municipal Golf Course. Open to the public and run also as a learning experience for Grand Canyon University students, the GCU Golf Course is a long (7,239 yards) and largely flat 18-hole course with plenty of shade. Maryvale Municipal Golf Course opened in 1961 and sometimes feels like a little older despite a $10-million renovation in 2016, but with greens fees well under $100 even with a cart, it's a popular course. Very close to both GCU Ballpark and American Family Fields of Phoenix. *Grand Canyon University Golf Course, 5902 W. Indian School Rd., Phoenix; 623/846-4022; **gcugolf.com**.*

Papago Golf Course is a classic old desert course, opening in 1963 and run by the city of Phoenix. It's now home to the Arizona State University golf program as well. *Papago Golf Course, 5595 E. Moreland St., Phoenix; 602/275-8428; **papagogolfcourse.com**.*

INSIDER'S TIP
Most high-end resorts, such as The Phoenician or the Arizona Biltmore, also sport golf courses for guests.

CHICAGO IN THE DESERT

With the White Sox and Cubs training in the Valley and plenty of Illinois expatriates on Arizona soil, there's a veritable Chicago vibe running through much of the Valley. No surprise that the Chicago roots are best shown through one of the best things about the Windy City: Food.

Throughout this book we'll note when there are brews with Chicago ties—Goose Island, Old Style, etc.—sold at ballparks, and we also note a few Chicago-based delicacies offered at and near Sloan Park. There are a few other reminders of Chicago on the culinary scene.

Rosati's Pizza (*rosatispizza.com*) can now be found

nationwide, but it still retains that Chicago charm, with the original location dating back to 1927. There are nine Rosati's Pizza locations throughout the Valley, including those in Peoria, Surprise, Glendale, and Tempe.

Similarly, the legendary Lou Malnati's (*loumalnatis.com*) has expanded nationwide, including locations in Phoenix, Tempe, and Scottsdale. Tip: the chain now offers tavern-style pies.

Portillo's has been expanding like mad, and that includes locations in Avondale, Scottsdale, and Tempe. The Tempe location is notable for Cubs fans, as it's just down the road from Sloan Park.

Interestingly, the best Chicago dog in Phoenix, according to many, may be found at a Phoenix area restaurant with no direct ties to the Windy City. The menu is dominated by Chicago delicacies at Chicago Hamburger (*3749 E. Indian School Rd., Phoenix; 602/955-4137; chicagohamburger.com*): Chicago dogs (Vienna Beef, of course) dragged through the garden, beef sandwiches, sliders, and more. Plenty of Chicago memorabilia on the walls, as well as more than a few Cubs logo placards.

INSIDER'S TIP

Several spring training ballparks sell Chicago-style dogs, some dragged through the garden. For those unacquainted with the phrase, dragged through the garden means a dog topped with yellow mustard, tomato slices, diced onions, neon-green relish, pickle spear, sport peppers, and celery salt, served on a poppy-seed bun. No, no ketchup.

BEER IN THE VALLEY

The natural accompaniment to baseball and spring training? Good beer. And it's a good day when you can combine outstanding beer with a sunny day at the ballpark. Whether it's a notable brew at the ballpark, a pregame brew at a watering spot near training camp, or a brewpub for a postgame dinner, you'll have plenty of great choices during your Cactus League trip.

We cover lots of brewpubs and breweries in the chapters covering specific training camps: proximity counts, of course. Here are some additional recommendations for worthy brewpubs and breweries. Some are in the suburbs far from spring-training camps, but unless you plan on spending eight hours a day in camp, you'll have time to drive to Chandler or Gilbert to hit one of these notable beer spots. In any case, the Valley of the Sun has transformed in the last ten or so years from a beer desert to a brewery oasis. Here are our choices for brewpubs and breweries worth the drive, in addition to the breweries and brewpubs listed elsewhere in this chapter. We also highlight beer outposts close to each of the 10 training camp ballparks.

We discuss Four Peaks plenty of times in the course of this book, but it's not an understatement to say the company has been a leader in the expansion of brewing in the Valley. The psychic center for this growth is the firm's original brewpub in Tempe, an easy drive from Sloan Park, Scottsdale Stadium, and Hohokam Stadium. You will be exposed to a lot of Four Peaks offerings during the course of spring training, as almost every spring-training venue sells their beers on draft or in cans. (In fact, you can find Four Peaks hospitality shaded bars at several ballparks.)

There are plenty of worthy alternatives to Four Peaks, however. Here is a list of our favorite watering holes, listed by city. The common denominator: these are all venues definitely worth a drive.

- SanTan Brewing Co. has multiple locations, including the flagship Chandler tap (*8 S. San Marcos Place, Chandler; 480/917-8700*) and Sky Harbor Airport (*Terminal 3, 3400 E. Sky Harbor Blvd Phoenix; 602/245-2832; santanbrewing.com*). You can find SanTan beer across the Valley and at spring-training ballparks.
- Arizona Wilderness Brewing Co. (*azwbeer.com*) has two locations in Gilbert (*721 N. Arizona Av., Gilbert; 480/284-9863*) and downtown Phoenix (*201 E. Roosevelt St., Phoenix; 480/462-1836*).
- Attic Ale House (*4247 E. Indian School Rd., Phoenix; 602/955-1967; theatticalehouseaz.com*). Check out the food as well.
- O.H.S.O. Brewery & Distillery (*15681 N. Hayden Rd., #112, Scottsdale, AZ 85260; 602/955-0358; ohsobrewery.com*), which also has a unique presence at Scottsdale Stadium. You can find O.H.S.O. products at a variety of brewpubs and bars.
- Grand Avenue Brewing Co. (*1205 W. Pierce St., Phoenix; 602/670-5465; grandavebrew.com*), in the downtown Phoenix area.
- SunUp Brewing Co. (*330 E. Camelback Rd., Phoenix; 602/279-8909; sunup.beer*).
- Wren House Brewing Co. (*2125 N. 24th St., Phoenix; 602/244-9184; wrenhousebrewing.com*). Remember earlier in this chapter when we discussed the small and modest neighborhood joints popping up across Phoenix? Wren House Brewing definitely falls under this category. The tap house is modest, to be

sure, with a small bar, one large communal table, and a few smaller tables. But the beer is great, the staff is friendly, and the atmosphere is chill. No big-screen TVs, no food; just high-quality beer.

- Huss Brewing Co. (*1520 W. Mineral Rd., Tempe; 480/264-7611; 100 E Camelback Rd., #160, Phoenix; 602/441.4677; hussbrewing.com*).
- The Perch (*232 S. Wall St., Chandler; 480/773-7688; perchpubbrewery.com*). The brewpub's courtyard features a collection of over 50 brightly colored, tropical rescue birds, and views of the area from a second-level rooftop bar. A little off the beaten path for many spring-training attendees, but worth the drive.
- Front Pourch Brewing (*1611 W. Whispering Wind Dr., Suite 7, Phoenix; 623/277-0526; frontpourchbrewing.com*). Try the Toasted Blonde if it's on tap.
- Fate Brewing (*4445 N. 7th St., Phoenix; 602/354-4700; 201 E. Southern Av., Tempe; 1312 N. Scottsdale Rd., Scottsdale; fatebrewing.com*).

We cover some other breweries and brewpubs close to the ballparks, but this should give you a good overview of the possibilities across the Valley.

AMERICAN FAMILY FIELDS OF PHOENIX / MILWAUKEE BREWERS

QUICK FACTS

- **Capacity**: 10,000, including berm seating
- **Year Opened**: 1998; renovated in 2019
- **Dimensions**: 350L, 395C, 340R
- **Dugout Location**: First-base side
- **Practice Times**: Gates open early, but practices don't start until approximately 10 a.m.
- **Gates Open**: Two hours before game time, but don't be surprised if you arrive at the ballpark and the gates aren't opened or they've been open for a half hour; the Brewers are notoriously casual about these things. Brewers BP, 11-11:50 a.m.
- **Ticket Line**: 800/933-7890
- **Address**: 3805 N. 53rd Av., Phoenix, AZ 85031
- **Directions**: Take 51st Avenue (Exit 139 off I-10) north for two miles. Turn left on Indian School Road, then take another left at Raising Canes.

AMERICAN FAMILY FIELDS: A PEACEFUL OASIS

It is a true neighborhood ballpark, reflecting the Maryvale area while also providing a first-class experience for both fans and players. The Brewers are a working-class team these days, and that organization attitude is reflected in American Family Fields of Phoenix, emerging from a major renovation in spring training 2019.

The ballpark and training complex had been largely untouched since it opened in 1998; yes, there had been some small improvements here and there in terms of training facilities and some cluttering of the concourse over time, but in general the former Maryvale Baseball Park was in sore need of TLC. The Brewers partnered with the city of Phoenix on the overdue upgrades. For the Brewers and the city, the investment in the training complex was more than an investment in baseball: it was also an investment in the Maryvale neighborhood, which certainly could use a boost.

Besides a financial investment, the renovated ballpark was designed to be more inviting to all on a year-round basis. So, after deciding to re-commit to Phoenix and American Family Fields of Phoenix, the team unveiled a plan to open the ballpark to the surrounding community. Instead of operating as a fortress within the Maryvale community, the configuration is designed to be more inviting. The goal of the renovations was to reorient the ballpark from an inward-looking facility to one better integrated with the Maryvale neighborhood.

The changes to American Family Fields of Phoenix are apparent upon arrival to the facility. The parking lots south of the training facility have been altered, and a new walkway from there to the ballpark features plenty of access to player workout facilities. The new configuration removed the small parking lot directly to the south of the ballpark and replaced it with new entrances (including a grand plaza), new workout facilities, and a smaller agility field. Part of parking east of the ballpark was lost to a new workout field.

Meanwhile, the entrances to the ballpark were over-hauled. A small entrance gate on the east side of the complex (down the right-field line) features its own ticket windows.

INSIDER'S TIP
Use these ticket window when you can. On a busy day you will likely encounter lines at the main ticket window and gate, but we've never encountered much in the way of delays at this side gate.

The showcase entrance at the aforementioned 25,000-square-foot plaza features displays honoring retired Brewers numbers and team history. With plenty of shade and native plants, this is the place to meet friends and family before the game.

In the past, this area behind home plate was closed off and cluttered with concessions. The concessions are gone, and the ballpark is now more inviting to the community.

Once inside, you'll find widened concourses, expanded concessions, enhanced signage, and a new, larger team store. In an ideal world, ballparks should open to a view of the field behind home plate, just for the drama involved— but practicality plays a large role here, as the back of the ballpark concourse blends into a grand plaza that can be used for all sorts of community events unrelated to baseball. That sort of space doesn't currently exist in the Maryvale area.

The entry plaza features the primary ticket office and gates to the ballpark, replacing the old entry gates in back of first base. The east side of the plaza area also includes the lobby entrance to the new clubhouse building. In addition, there is an entry to the new retail store from outside of the home plate gate, allowing fans access to the store during non-game times.

Fans will notice a standalone two-story building running between the home-plate gate and the right-field corner. This building houses clubhouses, training spaces, expanded training spaces and medical facilities, support functions for the Major and Minor League teams, a flagship retail sales store, and a primary ticket office at the new home plate gate. The building serves fans both at the widened concourse level with concessions and restrooms, and team office space on the other side. The second floor sports offices for Baseball Operations and features a walkout patio with views of training facilities to the south.

One potential downside of this upgrade: games at American Family Fields of Phoenix are more popular, with attendance per game increasing in recent years. Giants and Cubs games always see a bump at the American Family Fields of

Phoenix gate, but the generally better numbers surely means more locals are making a Brewers ballpark run.

And no matter where your team allegiances lie, you'll find American Family Fields of Phoenix to be a very pleasant place to take in a baseball game. Despite its name, the training complex is within Phoenix city limits; Maryvale is a neighborhood in western Phoenix, bumping up against Glendale. There's plenty of space surrounding the ballpark, as well as ample seating within.

There are some pleasant aspects to American Family Fields of Phoenix carried past the 2019 renovations. As noted, there's a lot of shade in the ballpark: a trellised canopy runs from just beyond third base to the right-field corner. The concessions from Delaware North are good: there is a decent beer selection (Miller brews, of course, including Miller High Life), and a concourse area featuring grills with burgers, brats, and the highly recommended chicken tenders. (We have found the $7 hot dog to be adequate, but a tad pricey.) The main concession stands offer brats, chorizo, and Polish sausages, as well as the unique Bratchos—Wisconsin-style kettle chips topped with bratwurst. There's a mandatory Bloody Mary stand as well as cheese curds—we are talking Sconnie fans, after all. Other hints of home include the familiar Sausage Race and a traditional "Roll Out the Barrel" in the middle of the seventh.

If you want shade, head to the concourse; a nice roof will give you relief from the sun. Need to stretch your legs? Take a hike around the 360-degree concourse, stopping for some liquid relief at one of the standalone concession stands in the left-field corner. No matter where you sit, you have easy access to concessions and you can stretch your legs throughout the course of a long game, and most fans don't need more than that. To avoid the sun, sit on the first-base side or in the right-field berm.

INSIDER'S TIP

If you are using a mapping application like Apple Maps or Google Maps to get you to the ballpark, be sure to have the 53rd Avenue address entered. The former main entrance was on 51st Avenue, and on a crowded day you may be routed back to that entrance.

In the past, American Family Fields of Phoenix was perfectly pleasant because the Brewers were not a strong draw. (One of the most common praises of the ballpark: it's great because there are no crowds to muck up the lines, and you can walk up to the ticket office and snare a great seat.) With the 2019 renovations, American Family Fields of Phoenix provides a much better fan experience—and the crowds have followed.

THE SPRING-TRAINING BALLPARK EXPERIENCE

CONCESSIONS

The renovations added more concessions stands to the mix, particularly in the new spaces along the right-field line. Those new stands led to a better food experience: concessions are now prepped at these stands and not prepared at a commissary before being carted to points of sale.

As with American Family Field (the former Miller Park), a mandatory food item for a Brewers game is a bratwurst, considered among the best in the Cactus League. The conventional approach is to top it with sauerkraut and spiced mustard, but be brave and try the Secret Stadium Sauce. It's a Milwaukee ballpark staple. The legend is that the concessionaire at the old County Stadium created it when facing a ketchup shortage, and it does have a barbecue sauce, ketchup, and mustard base, but it's hard to discern any other secret ingredients from the bottles for sale at American Family Field gift shops. Maybe Worcestershire sauce? In the past, at American Family Fields of Phoenix, the aforementioned bottles are placed at a few condiment stations in the concourse. This being the spring home of the Milwaukee Brewers, there are also several other wursts, chorizo, and dogs available.

And, of course, there is Miller High Life (our fave), Miller Lite, Blue Moon, Blue Moon Wit, and Blue Moon Peach Ale on tap in past years. Bombers of Corona, Pacifico, Modelo, and Heineken are also available. (Don't like beer? Try the canned gin and tonic.)

Being a Wisconsin team, the Brewers and the team's concessionaire couldn't help but bring in a few local delicacies. Deep-fried cheese curds, a staple in many Milwaukee and Madison restaurants, are now available. You can get those curds on top of a Wisconsin Curd Burger, along with hot sauce. Also available: Bratchos, hot kettle chips covered in nacho cheese and slices of bratwurst. (Yes, hot chips—warmed-up potato chips—are very Sconnie.) BBQ Mac and Cheese and Buffalo Chicken Nachos, topped with chicken and buffalo sauce, round out the indulgent offerings.

On a hot day, a frozen banana or a shaved ice can be refreshing. Also recommended by many fans: kettle corn.

No matter if you're a longtime Brewers spring-training attendee or an American Family Fields of Phoenix newbie, you'll want to take the time to check things out before buying that first Miller High Life of the spring.

AUTOGRAPHS

There's no designated autograph area at American Family Fields of Phoenix, so your best bet is to arrive early to the ballpark and attract the attention of the players as they head from the clubhouse to the field. Brewers enter the field from a clubhouse entrance down the right-field line and will congregate near the home dugout. A visitors clubhouse in the left-field corner means players enter by crossing a roped-off concourse and walking down to the field. They also exit the game via the same route, but they typically don't stop.

INSIDER'S TIP
This being a spring outpost for Sconnies, there is the obligatory Sausage Race in the middle of the sixth inning and the playing of "Roll Out the Barrel" after "Take Me Out to the Ballgame" in the seventh-inning stretch. In the past, the participants in the Sausage Race would sign autographs on the concourse near Section 117 after their racing exploits.

One nice touch: there's definitely a relaxed vibe at American Family Fields of Phoenix, a vibe that seems to infect opposing teams as well. You'll usually find both teams milling around their dugout before a game, and both coaching staffs will engage in friendly chats with fans. As an organization, the Brewers have cultivated openness with the fans, and that attitude is certainly on display at American Family Fields of Phoenix.

The entrance to the clubhouse is down the right-field line, so home players must walk in foul territory after leaving the game. This is the place to buy a ticket and try to snare an autograph before or after the game.

Another game plan: attend morning practice. The Brewers open workouts at 10 a.m. in the adjoining practice fields. You can try to snare a player heading to or from workouts.

INSIDER'S TIP

If the Brewers have scheduled an away game and you're really itching for a star player's signature, head to the practice facility at 9 a.m. The gates to the ballpark are open for batting practice, and the team allows fans to watch before the team departs at 10 a.m.

PARKING

Your choices are to either pay $10 to park at the complex (there's a large grassy field between the ballpark and 51st Avenue, with a small paved area closer to the ballpark) or take your chances parking in the surrounding area, which presents its own set of issues. Some park in the adjoining Maryvale Plaza and walk over, though the team warns against it. (When there's a large crowd, you're diverted to the nearby Wal-Mart for parking. Be warned it does not take a sellout to fill the American Family Fields of Phoenix parking lots, so arrive early if a popular team like the Cubs or Giants is in town.) The advice: bite the bullet and pay for the parking. The city and the Brewers do sweeten the deal with a free shuttle running between the ballpark and the parking lots. As with Miller Park, the Brewers encourage tailgating, so come extra early (gates open three hours before gametime) and grab a paved spot for some Sconnie-style pregame festivities.

The Brewers also encourage ridesharing to and from the ballpark. The drop-off area is off 53rd Avenue, by the main gates.

WHERE TO SIT

For most games you'll have a pretty solid selection of seats. The Brewers dugout is on the first-base side between Sections 105 and 113. The visitors dugout is on the third-base side between Sections 106 and 114. If there's a real character leading the opposition, sitting next to the visitor dugout can be a more interesting experience.

INSIDER'S TIP
You can find the most shade in the back half of most seating sections as well as the berm in right field.

There were some other subtle upgrades to the seating bowl. Gone are the bleachers down each line, replaced by new seating that matches the existing theater-style ballpark seating.

Berm seating means a relaxing time in the outfield. Both bullpens are located in the outfield-berm area, so you can get up-close and personal with both sets of relief pitchers.

SELFIE SPOTS

The old Maryvale Baseball Park lacked any decent selfie spots. The grand plaza is the best place to score a selfie, next to the oversized numbers honoring retired numbers. Another good selfie if he's at the ballpark: a Brewer Beer Barrel Man mascot greeting fans right inside the front gates.

IF YOU GO

WHAT TO DO OUTSIDE THE BALLPARK

The Maryvale neighborhood is not one of the more upscale areas of Phoenix. However, the area just north of the ballpark —51st Avenue and Indian School Road—has been built up in recent years and now sports a string of decent fast-food options, in case you want to grab an early lunch before the ballgame. Your choices include Presto Pizza (highly recommended), Wendy's, Subway, Wingstop, Denny's, and Pizza Hut, and the trendy Raising Cane's Chicken Fingers chain.

There's also an abundance of small taco and tortas shops, including the well-regarded Los Reyes de la Torta (*4333 W. Indian School Rd., Phoenix; 602/269-3212; losreyesdelatortaphx.com*). Tortas are basically Mexican hamburgers, with meats and cheeses stuffed between bolillo rolls (basically French bread). It's takeout-only at Los Reyes de la Torta, so grab a bag and head early to the ballpark for a little Sconnie-style tailgating. If you're a golfer, you can get in nine or 18 holes at the nearby Grand Canyon University Golf Course (*5902 W. Indian School Rd., Phoenix; 623/846-4022; gcugolf.com*), renovated at the beginning of 2018.

You don't need to head far from the Indian School Road/51st Avenue area to find some great food. If you are a fan of Vietnamese beef noodle soup, better known as pho, we'd recommend Pho 43 Express (*2844 N. 43rd Av., Phoenix; 602/269-3383*), though the steamed egg meatloaf is worth a try. Also east of the ballpark: Ta'Carbon (*2929 N. 43rd Av., Phoenix; 602/682-7701; tacarbon.com*), serving Sonoran-style tacos filled with various meats, including carne asada and beef *lengua*. (*Lengua*, of course, is tongue. Highly underrated.)

One of the great secrets of Phoenix is the vast number of sports and dive bars throughout the Valley. The legendary Max's is closed, but at Hail Mary's Sports Bar (*formerly the Westside Cocktail Lounge, 5114 W. Camelback Rd., Glendale; 623/934-1780*), there's really no pretense about watching sports: this is a place to take in a $3 macrobrews shortly after the 9 a.m. opening. Be warned: it's a cash-only establishment.

Speaking of Glendale: you are close to the charms of that up-and-coming suburb. We cover Glendale in our Camelback Ranch–Glendale chapter, and it's only a 20-minute drive from the ballpark to the Westgate Entertainment District, which we discuss at length. One of our favorite sushi joints in the Valley of the Sun is a short drive away: Moto (*6845 N. 16th St., Phoenix; 602/263-5444;* **mrmotorising.com**) at the corner of 16th and Glendale. Great sushi and a great selection of beer.

Downtown Glendale has its own attractions, and it's only four or so miles from the ballpark. Glendale is not exactly party central, but it does have its own charms: antique lovers flock to the many antique shops in downtown Glendale, while anyone with a sweet tooth appreciates a tour of Cerreta Candy Company, which offers tours Monday-Friday. Yes, any chocolate-factory tour is merely an excuse to devour samples at the end, and the Cerreta Candy products are worth the wait: French mints, milk and dark chocolates, caramels, truffles, crunches, and nut clusters. *Cerreta Candy Company, 5345 W. Glendale Av., Glendale; 623/930-9000;* **cerreta.com**.

If you didn't get your fill of brats at the ballpark, there's a pretty decent German restaurant nearby: Haus Murphy's, which features the requisite pretzels, sausages, kraut, schnitzel, rouladen, and accordion player. *Haus Murphy's, 5739 W. Glendale Av., Glendale; 623/939-2480;* **hausmurphys.com**.

Also in downtown Glendale: La Piazza Al Forno, which offers an outstanding white pizza. A change of pace from the ballpark food dominating your diet. *La Piazza Al Forno, 5803 W. Glendale Av., Glendale; 623/847-3301.*

Also relatively close: GCU Ballpark, which was extensively rebuilt for the 2018 and 2019 NCAA seasons. The Grand Canyon University campus is four miles or so away from American Family Fields of Phoenix, and we'd recommend a day-night doubleheader if the schedule allows. (We cover it in our college-baseball chapter.) Plus, you are in the western edge of Phoenix, which means you're close to Peoria and the rest of the West Valley. Check out our chapters on Peoria Stadium, Surprise Stadium, Camelback Ranch–Glendale, and Goodyear Ballpark for more information on what to do in those areas.

WHERE TO STAY

There really is no reason to stay near American Family Fields of Phoenix. There are no attractions in the surrounding neighborhood, no hot and trendy restaurants in the area, and no hotels within walking distance. You will find some hotels close to I-10 within a few miles of the ballpark (in the city's Midtown area), but we're not talking about plush and scenic resorts: we're talking Super 8, Motel 6, and Red Roof Inn, all sitting next to the freeway, to boot.

> **INSIDER'S TIP**
>
> There was no official team hotel for 2024. Instead, look at staying either in nearby Glendale or downtown Phoenix. Glendale is a suburb located north and west of the Maryvale neighborhood, between Phoenix and Peoria. It's the spring home of the Los Angeles Dodgers and Chicago White Sox. It's also home to Desert Diamond Arena, a busy concert venue, as well as State Farm Stadium, home of the NFL's Arizona Cardinals. There is a cluster of hotels in the Westgate Entertainment District next to the arena.

We discuss some other hotspots in the greater Glendale area in our Camelback Ranch–Glendale chapter. There has been a lot of new development in the area—though very little close to the ballpark itself—and staying in the general area will both give you access to some great ballparks as well as good restaurants and accommodations in the Goodyear/Glendale/Peoria freeway corridor.

SPRING-TRAINING HISTORY: MILWAUKEE BREWERS

If there's a Major League Baseball team strongly associated with spring training—at least historically—it's the Milwaukee Brewers, literally born during the last days of spring training in 1970. The Brewers franchise began life as the Seattle Pilots during the 1969 season. It was a rush job: MLB had not planned on expanding until 1972 or so, but political pressure from Missouri politicians after Charlie Finley fled to Oakland with the Athletics led baseball to expand in Kansas City and Seattle ahead of schedule. MLB had been working on a new-ballpark plan for Seattle, but with the hasty decision to expand, all the work done on that new ballpark—which eventually became the Kingdome—was temporarily put aside. That put the Pilots playing out of Sick's Stadium, a former Minor League Baseball ballpark that opened in 1938 and had seen much better days before being hastily expanded during the 1969 season.

INSIDER'S TIP
Interestingly, this was not the first time Milwaukee baseball fans were rewarded with an MLB team during spring training. After months of speculation, Boston Braves owner Lou Perini announced on March 13, 1953 that he would seek permission to move his team to Milwaukee and the brand-new Milwaukee County Stadium. Permission was granted by MLB owners on March 18, and the team set attendance records in Milwaukee before interest faded and the team was moved once again, this time to Atlanta.

Everything about that 1969 season was temporary: on Opening Day Sick's Stadium had a capacity of 17,000 or so, and it wasn't until June that the ballpark's capacity reached

25,420—far short of the 30,000 capacity mandated by Major League Baseball when the Pilots expansion franchise was awarded. The Pilots ended the season in some deep debt (owing $3.5 million to Bank of California, $1 million to stockholders, $165,000 for the Sick's Stadium lease, $250,000 to the American League for dues, among others), so the owners—Pacific Northwest Sports, with Dewey and Max Soriano controlling 34 percent of the shares—sought to sell the team to Milwaukee Brewers Baseball Club, Inc., a group led by local car dealer/fleet manager Allan "Bud" Selig, a former Milwaukee Braves minority investor who would become MLB commissioner in 1992.

That sale was opposed in court by the city of Seattle, King County, and a local group seeking to keep the Pilots at Sick's Stadium. The drama played out throughout 1970 spring training, as talk of a team move to County Stadium dominated the headlines and distracted the players training at Tempe Diablo Stadium. MLB had already approved a move to Milwaukee, and prototype Brewers uniforms (showing a Boston Red Sox-style uniform script, which was never used) surfaced on the wires in the midst of spring training. In the end, Federal Bankruptcy Referee Sidney C. Volinn approved the sale of the Pilots to Selig and crew on March 30, 1970, just a week before the regular season began.

CAMELBACK RANCH-GLENDALE / CHICAGO WHITE SOX / LOS ANGELES DODGERS

QUICK FACTS

- **Capacity**: 13,000 (10,300 fixed seats, plus berm and standing room)
- **Year Opened**: 2009
- **Dimensions**: 345L, 385LC, 410C, 385RC, 345R
- **Dugout Locations**: Dodgers on the third-base side, White Sox on the first-base side
- **Practice Times**: Gates open at 9 a.m., with practices starting around 9:30 a.m.
- **Gates Open**: 60 minutes before game time, but gates to the center-field courtyard, as well as concessions and team stores, open at 10:30 a.m. on game days. Home batting practice, until 11:05 a.m.; visitors batting practice, 11:05 a.m.-12:05 p.m.; home infield, 12:10-12:20 p.m.; visitors infield, 12:20-12:30 p.m. Add six hours for a night game.
- **Ticket Lines**: 602/302-5000
- **Address**: 10710 W. Camelback Rd., Phoenix, AZ 85037

- **Directions**: Take the Loop 101 (Agua Fria Loop) to the Camelback Road exit. Turn west to the ballpark. If there's a large crowd expected, Glendale authorities will advise a different exit and route to the ballpark, especially if you are coming in from the north. Watch for the signs posted on the 101.

ONE WITH NATURE IN GLENDALE

When visiting Camelback Ranch–Glendale, spring home of the Dodgers and White Sox, definitely wear your walking shoes. Yes, it's possible to just head straight to your seats from the parking lot and watch the game, but you'd miss out on so much. As one of the most pleasant spring-training complexes in the Valley, Camelback Ranch–Glendale provides plenty of great memory-making moments for fans old and young.

Located on the west side of the Valley, Camelback Ranch–Glendale is designed to appear to rise from the flat local terrain. A symmetrical two-building outpost in center field houses the main ticket office, the large team store, and other operations. The curved buildings immediately set the tone for the spring experience at Camelback Ranch–Glendale.

The place is made for strolling. You are welcome to meander through the training complex before reaching the game, watching multiple workouts on multiple diamonds. The experience is then topped with a game at one of the nicest ballparks in spring training.

But a spring-training complex must also fulfill all the needs of the main tenants. Both teams have state-of-the-art training facilities for their major- and minor-league squads, allowing both to smoothly run year-round operations. Fans don't see what happens behind the scenes. Most won't find things like weight rooms, aquatic treadmills, and multiple clubhouses very sexy or interesting. And if you're truly interested in how an MLB team runs spring training, you'll want to read how both teams set up their operations spaces for their specific needs. The White Sox chose to put minor- and major-league facilities in the same building, though there are some differences in each section. The Dodgers, meanwhile, chose to break out the minor-league operations in a three-building complex, with separate buildings for training, support, and clubhouses. As with any modern training facility, there's video through the entire complex, giving coaches the chance to provide instant feedback to position players and pitchers. Nutrition is monitored in cafeterias, while plenty of workout fields allow for minor league games, specific drills and more. As a fan, you won't see the hydro pools or the clubhouses, but you'll have a chance to arrive early to stroll the grounds and see the hard work associated with spring training in action.

The Glendale spring-training complex is one of the largest in the majors. The site, organized around a central connecting path and three-acre lake, hosts two ballpark entries—one at home plate and a more prominent entry at center field. (We recommend entering via the center-field gates if you can. More on that later.) Located on a 141-acre site, the ballpark has the capacity to host 13,500 fans. It includes more than 118,000 square feet of major- and minor-league clubhouses as well as four major-league practice fields, eight minor-league practice fields, and two practice infields. Each team has a replica major-league field to emulate their home ballpark.

Most fans will enter the ballpark at the parking lot located at West Camelback Road and 107th Avenue, west of the Camelback/I-101 interchange. This 1,000-plus-space parking lot is behind the grandstand. You'll need to walk around the perimeter to make your way to the practice field if you end up parking behind home plate, as MLB entry rules bar entering the ballpark and then re-entering.

From the center-field entry facing out from the ballpark, the White Sox training complex is on the right and the Dodgers' complex on the left. Each team has two MLB fields and four minor-league fields, as well as a half infield and specialized areas for sliding and bunting drills. A five-acre-plus water feature (connected lake, river, and pond), stocked with fish, separates the two training areas. Besides serving as a holding pond for reclaimed water destined for watering the grounds, the pond serves an aesthetic function: there's nothing more soothing than running water. Paths branch out from roughly the center of the complex to each team's MLB-sized practice fields.

The 141-acre site isn't purely symmetric, reflecting each team's approach to player development. On the White Sox side, you have nothing but training fields. The main MLB field has limited access, with fans kept a distance from the players. On the Dodgers side, the main MLB practice field is almost totally open to fans. While there's seating (but no

shade) at both practice fields, it's pretty clear the Dodgers
want to encourage players to interact with fans—at least more
than the White Sox brain trust does, for now. The Dodgers
have also spent more time upgrading their part of the
training area. Dodger greats are honored with large baseballs
decorated with their names. Two large scoreboards in the
shape of the iconic Dodger Stadium outfield scoreboards
provide daily information.

INSIDER'S TIP
Head to the area outside of the left-field wall of the
replica Dodger Stadium practice field. There you'll
find orange, grapefruit, and lemon groves—tributes to
the historic Dodgertown training complex (which we
discuss later in this chapter), Southern California, and
Arizona.

As a fan, you're free to roam around most of the training

complex. The clubhouses are off limits—which is too bad, because they're gorgeous—and typically some of the practice fields are blocked off as well. Still, in terms of access, this is one of the most open spring complexes we've ever visited.

INSIDER'S TIP
Technically, Camelback Ranch–Glendale is in the Phoenix city limits, though it was built by Glendale. The land is owned by Glendale and was acquired from Phoenix originally to protect Glendale Municipal Airport from encroachment. But the ballpark's address is Phoenix.

A symmetrical two-building outpost in center field houses the main ticket office, the large team store, and other operations. The curved buildings immediately set the tone for the spring experience at Camelback Ranch–Glendale: the 14 buildings comprising the complex were designed to appear to rise from the flat Valley floor, with sloping roofs, asymmetrical designs, and organic appearances. It also sits slightly off the trees in back of the batter's eye, giving fans a view of the field and home plate as they approach the field of play.

The ballpark seats 13,500 (10,500 fixed seats, the remainder on the berm, plus standing room), but it feels smaller. Though the complex is set on 141 acres, the ballpark takes up a small part of that, and the combination of below-grade playing field and surrounding outbuildings carves out an intimate space. The theme throughout the ballpark is focused on natural materials and finishes; besides the gabion walls so prominent in the outfield concourse, the buildings have a stone or brown finish, and the outbuildings feature angled roofs designed to feel like a natural part of the desert skyline. The seats are done in a desert brown; surrounded by so many neutrals and browns, the green grass is especially resplendent. And the foliage within the ballpark has nicely grown out: the trees are taller and cover more ground, while the climate-specific plants (cacti, shrubs, flowers) look like they have been there forever.

The suite/press box deck in back of home plate fits in with that aesthetic as well. W-shaped supports give it a gentle rise over the concourse, providing needed shade as well. In an interesting twist, eight suites are mini-suites, seating only six and sharing a buffet area. You can upgrade your tickets or directly buy access to the Legends Deck, which features lots of shade on the second deck, an all-you-can-eat buffet of ballpark food, and a private bar. (You can purchase the upgrade at the gates depending on availability.) Teams are finding that spring training is less about the large corporate outings and more about smaller gatherings with friends and close business acquaintances.

As you sit in the grandstand, you'll see two buildings down each line. Down the first-base line is the White Sox clubhouse/training facility, and down the third-base line is the Dodgers major-league clubhouse. Both teams enter the field from the clubhouses, albeit in slightly different ways: the White Sox enter from a truck entrance, while the Dodgers enter through a small tunnel under the outfield concourse and through the bullpen. You're able to see each team from the concourse, but you are not very close to the players.

When the game starts, take a good look at the second floor of the outfield buildings past the wraparound concourse, because that's where team officials will be. The Dodgers ownership commands a large suite and deck on the center-field side of the Los Angeles building, while White Sox owner Jerry Reinsdorf has a smaller suite and deck on the center-field side of his building. The executive offices are spacious, but not sumptuous; both teams use the complexes as year-round training and development facilities, so the office space is needed.

In many ways the ballpark was designed to be low-impact. Gabion walls will probably confound visitors upon their first visit to the ballpark, but they fit in the design aesthetic. Gabion walls are retaining walls made of stacked stones enmeshed by wire; the wire keeps the rocks from scattering, and the weight of the stones makes for an efficient retaining wall. You'll find gabion walls throughout the outfield concourse at Camelback Ranch–Glendale. Also, the fields throughout the complex are watered with reclaimed water from a local wastewater facility.

Much of what makes the complex unique, sad to say, is out of view for most fans. The complex is designed to be a working facility, as the business of baseball now requires a 12-month approach to the game. Each team has separate, but basically equal training facilities, adapted for each team's needs. We cannot imagine a situation that wouldn't be addressed by one specialized space or another, whether it's the underwater treadmills in the hydrotherapy rooms, the spacious therapy rooms, the many media rooms, the plethora of meeting rooms, or the various video rooms. Both franchises field teams in the rookie Arizona Complex League, and both send players to rehab under team supervision. And, of course, both teams are hoping players will settle in Phoenix in the winter and take advantage of the complex's workout facilities, batting cages, and more.

If you go, be prepared to make a day of it. You'll want to give yourself plenty of time to meander your way through the complex before the game, and it will take some time to make your way back to your car after the game. But go: Camelback Ranch–Glendale is one of the most scenic spring-training experiences in all of baseball.

INSIDER'S TIP
Yes, Camelback Ranch–Glendale has free WiFi.

INSIDER'S TIP
Plan on an early trip for Dodgers spring training. The team will open the MLB season in Tokyo on March 18 against the Cubs, which means an earlier reporting date, a Feb. 20 start to games, and a March 11 (!) end to Cactus League play.

THE SPRING-TRAINING BALLPARK EXPERIENCE

CONCESSIONS

Lots of good meat-based products can be found at Camelback Ranch–Glendale: brats, Dodger Dogs, Vienna Beef Chicago Dogs, Sonoran Dogs (wrapped in bacon and topped with salsa and sour cream), sausages, hamburgers, chili cheese fries, pizza, tamales, etc. A third-base-line stand offers a range of Mexican foods, a Wok-Off Noodles stand offers noodle bowls, and a right-field stand offers a variety of foot-longs—Sonoran Dogs, brats, and Italian sausages—as well as an Beyond vegan brat as well as the requisite onion, pepper, and sauerkraut toppings.

More hearty fare is available as well. Start with the barbeque cart behind home plate. It's served in a variety of ways, including a helmet filled with mac and cheese and topped with brisket. (Mac and cheese is also available served in a helmet at the Sausage Grill.) The legendary 18-inch pizza slice is big enough for two.

The beer selection runs the gamut between corporate brews and microbrews from the likes of Sam Adams, Goose Island, and Pyramid. Worth a trip: the Estrella Jalisco Patio in the right-field corner. Plenty of seating is offered both at the bar and in adjoining tables, and a large canopy provides shade for all. Lots of fans split their time between their seats and the beer garden. If your tastes run to something mixed, margaritas and other cocktails are served at the Estrella Jalisco Patio and the third-base-side Three Amigos Bar.

The big thing about the food at Camelback Ranch–Glendale: it's not necessarily the quality (though a day with a Dodger Dog is a good day indeed, even if they're no longer made by Farmer John), it's the accessibility. You're never too far from a concession stand or mobile point of sale. You are allowed to bring in an unopened water bottle and food in sealed packages. Our advice: freeze that water bottle and let it slowly melt in the warm Arizona air at the ballpark.

INSIDER'S TIP
The Montejo Patio features a shaded area with plenty of food and drink options, including bacon on a stick, pizza, kebobs, beer, and frozen margaritas.

INSIDER'S TIP
Some of the best seats at the ballpark were the open four tops past the berm in left field. These four tops are now covered and sold as the all-you-can-eat Bullpen Patio. With the umbrellas, you're not fighting the sun, giving you a really good view of the action on the field. Pricing is dependent on the day and the opponent, but you'll see a large placard at the box office offering Bullpen Patio tickets and upgrades if available.

AUTOGRAPHS

With so much access to the training fields and two teams committed to accessibility, you will have plenty of opportunities to approach a player for a signature. Wandering the grounds before the game (get there at 9 a.m. during early workouts, when players are hitting the fields) will yield some autograph opportunities from players from both teams, even if their team is not scheduled to play that day. Before the game, players from both teams will appear down the line and sign with no prompting from fans. After the game you'll find plenty of players approaching the stands for autographs as well.

PARKING

One word: *free*. It does require a little planning. A good reason to come early to the ballpark: you can avoid the long lines of fans entering the parking lots. Camelback Road was widened to four lanes when the ballpark was under construction, but it wasn't enough. Crowds at Camelback Ranch–Glendale are notoriously late to arrive—especially those Dodgers fans!—so getting there early is the best way to avoid the Camelback Road traffic.

The parking situation at Camelback Ranch–Glendale has changed over the years. Originally the main parking lot was meant to be the south lot, pushing fans to stroll through the training facility to get to the ballpark. In practice, most fans didn't want a leisurely stroll through the training fields and instead wanted to go directly to the ballpark, serviced by the west parking lot. So now the west and north parking lots are the main parking lots, and the south lot is used when there is a large crowd expected. If you want the full spring-training experience, park to the south (to your right as you enter the complex, technically Lot 1P) or to the north (technically Lot 3) and walk in through the complex. It's a stroll that puts you next to the training fields, the lovely pond, and the baseball history. Personally, we prefer the long stroll through the training camp—but we understand if you don't.

Many of you will now enter the ballparks via Ballpark Boulevard, which now extends north of the training complex, instead of dead-ending there. The extension is five lanes at the ballpark, providing some relief to area residents as well. By going north and turning into Maryland Avenue, you have easy access in and out from the Westgate Entertainment District northeast of the ballpark, at the 101/Glendale Avenue interchange. Many of you will look at staying, dining, or drinking at the nearby Westgate Entertainment District, so we cover it later in this chapter.

INSIDER'S TIP
When a large crowd is expected, fans will be directed to the south lot, resulting in some long lines in the right-hand lane. Zip around them in the left lane and head to Ballpark Boulevard. Hang a right and head to the west parking-lot entrances, where there will almost certainly be shorter lines.

INSIDER'S TIP
There are ticket windows located off both main entrances. You can pick up Will Call tickets at any window.

WHERE TO SIT

Because of the grandstand orientation, fans in the grandstand are facing southeast, as opposed to the traditional northeast. That cuts down on opportunities to find a seat out of the sun. New shade canopies down the first-base line means the last 14 rows in Sections 110-117, as well as the very last rows of other nearby 100-level sections, will be covered with shade at the beginning of the game, with the shade extending forward as the game goes along. (Let's hope some more canopies are installed down the third-base line in the future.) The second-level overhang extends to cover the very last rows of other nearby 100-level sections. The ballpark is also built for breezes: on a typical Arizona day, you'll enjoy some cooling zephyrs the closer you are to the concourse.

If you're not in a shaded seat, put on your sunscreen before you enter the ballpark, bring in a tube (spray cans are not allowed in the ballpark) or buy some in a team store. As a plus, there are no bleachers at Camelback Ranch–Glendale: every seat is a stadium-style seat.

If you find yourself in a sunny seat, take some breaks and walk the concourse. It's shaded and worth a break from the sun.

INSIDER'S TIP
The teams offer a senior (55+) discount on Mondays through Wednesdays. You may not even have to ask for it; it was offered out of the blue during our last paid visit to the ballpark.

INSIDER'S TIP
Depending on the day and the opponent, tickets are offered in three price levels: Bronze, Silver, and Gold, with ticket prices running $10 more from the lowest category to the highest for the same seat—even the lawn seating.

INSIDER'S TIP
Sections are numbered clockwise, beginning in the right-field corner and extended to the left-field corner. To sit near the White Sox dugout, go for Sections 5-11; to sit near the Dodgers dugout, go for Sections 19-25.

For a great view of the South Mountains, sit on the third-base side.

INSIDER'S TIP

The Legends Deck is sold as a group space. If it is not taken by a group, it's available as a game-day purchase priced between $40 and $80. It's a fully shaded area with comfortable seating and all-you-can-eat buffet.

One interesting area created in recent years: the left-field Bullpen Patio, featuring an all-you-can-eat buffet and shaded four tops. You'll have a great view of the Dodgers bullpen.

Camelback Ranch–Glendale sports one of the largest berm areas in all of baseball, easily accommodating 3,000 folks. On a typical sunny afternoon, your best bet is sitting in the right-field area: you won't be staring into the sun. But there will be a drawback to some berm seating: you won't be able to see the high-def right-center scoreboard.

INSIDER'S TIP

One place with a decent vantage in the outfield berm: against the gabion fence in back of the White Sox bullpen. The gabion fence provides some shade, and unless there are a lot of gawkers peering into the bullpen, your view of the field will be clear.

INSIDER'S TIP

If you're at the ballgame by yourself and want a place to hang out with a cold beer in hand, we recommend two SRO areas: on the concourse behind home plate (in the shade, natch) or in the left-field berm.

One other huge plus for Camelback Ranch–Glendale: it is one of the most physically accessible ballparks in all of spring training. Everyone enters at ground level, and there's an accessible ramp located down the third-base line next to section 128 for those needing to get to lower areas of seating. ADA seating is located throughout the concourse, including platforms above sections 3, 4, 11, 15, 26, 27, 102, 103, 104, 106, 107, 108 (if not used by a TV crew), 112, 118, 121, 123 (if not used by a TV crew), 124, 126, 127, and 128.

Some fans love sitting near the bullpens. For your planning purposes: the Dodgers bullpen is in the left-field corner in front of the berm, the White Sox bullpen is in the right-field corner in front of the berm. You can get close to the White Sox bullpen from the berm—handy for autograph seekers before and after the game—but the berm layout keeps fans a fair distance away from the Dodgers bullpen. As a bonus, both bullpens now sport the retired numbers of players.

INSIDER'S TIP
If you go, plan ahead. Camelback Ranch–Glendale tacks a $5 surcharge on tickets bought the day of the game.

SELFIE SPOTS

The larger-than-life Tommy Lasorda and Frank Thomas bobbleheads are big hits with fans seeking the perfect ballpark selfie. They're located in the center-field plaza, easily accessible to all. There are also great spots outside the ballpark proper in the training area. In general, the water feature with the baseballs honoring Dodgers greats, the giant LA logo, and the miniature Dodgervision scoreboards are popular places to congregate and snap selfies before the game. Guideposts featuring the team's Minor League Baseball affiliates and the distance to their home ballparks can be found in the center-field plaza area inside the gates.

IF YOU GO

WHAT TO DO OUTSIDE THE BALLPARK

Development was supposed to accompany the ballpark, but a bad economy scared off investors, so the ballpark is somewhat of an island in Glendale. There is not much within walking distance of the ballpark yet, save lots of housing developments. And, in fact, more housing is coming to the west of the ballpark.

The 101/Camelback Road interchange features a slew of fast-food joints of the national variety as well as a few unique offerings. On the fast-food front, we'd recommend the In-and-Out Burger (*9585 W. Camelback Rd.*) or Culver's (*5127 N. 99th Av.*) for something you can't necessarily find at home. Another cluster of restaurants can be found south of the ball-park at the Indian School Road/N. 107th Av. interchange, but the offerings here are geared more toward unique mom-and-pop outlets with offerings ranging from barbecue and Greek to tortas and sushi. For some sports-bar action after you've spent too much time in the sun, check out Ric's Sports Grille (*5134 N. 95th Av., Glendale; 623/594-0900; ricson95th.com*), across the freeway from the ballpark.

Many of you will head for the Westgate Entertainment District northeast of the ballpark at the 101/Glendale Avenue interchange. Anchored by Desert Diamond Arena (former home of the NHL's Arizona Coyotes) and State Farm Stadium (home of the NFL's Arizona Cardinals), the Westgate Entertainment District features a slew of bars, restaurants, movie theaters, and retail. We're a fan of the local State 48 brewery chain, and it's at Westgate Entertainment District where you will find a Glendale outpost, State 48 Funk House Brewery (*6770 N. Sunrise Blvd., Glendale; 623/877-4448; state48brewery.com*). The menu is heavy on wheat beers and golden ales, perfect for a hot Arizona day. Wicked Wolf (*9425 W. Coyotes Blvd., Glendale; 623/872-0022; wickedwolfglendale.com*) is the successor to a notable Westgate Entertainment hotspot (McFadden's), with plenty of big-screen TVs and drink specials after afternoon games and a rocking DJ-boosted dance floor later in the evening. Our favorites also include Yard House Glendale (*9401 W. Westgate Blvd., Glendale; 623/872-3900; yardhouse.com*), a sports bar with a long beer list, a surprisingly good menu, and notable Happy Hour. In fact, you won't lack for sports bars in the area in case you want to check out March Madness, as you'll also find a Buffalo Wild Wings (*9404 W. Westgate Blvd., Glendale; 623/877-9127; buffalowildwings.com*) and Dave & Buster's (*9460 W. Hanna Lane, Glendale; 623/759-7800; daveandbusters.com*). Another place to catch some March Madness, this time while enjoying a good cigar: Fine Ash Cigars (*9380 W. Westgate Blvd., Suite D-107, Glendale; 623/900-4752; fineashcigars.com*).

All in all, there are 45 bars and restaurants in the complex, ranging from Bar Louie and Salt Tacos and Tequila to Cold Stone Creamery and Johnny Rockets. Head there after the game for the many Happy Hours, dinner, and a flick. The place has grown from nothing several years ago to a genuinely hopping area on most nights, especially when a big act is playing the arena. *Westgate Entertainment District, 6751 N. Sunset Blvd.; Glendale; 623/385-7502;* **westgateaz.com**.

If you want a quieter venue, head farther north to Northern Avenue and the renovated Park West complex, and you'll encounter another set of great restaurants, including a Fleming's Steakhouse (*9712 W. Northern Av., Peoria; 623/772-9463;* **flemingssteakhouse.com**); The Cabin Whiskey and Grill (*9868 W. Northern Av., Peoria; 623/772-5974;* **cabinwest.com**), especially at Happy Hour; and a Grimaldi's Pizzeria (*9788 W. Northern Av. Peoria; 623/486-4455;* **grimaldispizzeria.com**).

You are also not far from the P83 Entertainment District surrounding Peoria Stadium. We cover it in more depth in our San Diego Padres/Seattle Mariners chapter. When the White Sox take on the Mariners or the Padres, a popular Chicago fan gathering spot before or after games is The Moon Saloon, with an abundance of beers, TVs, and March Madness devotees. It's part of the P83 entertainment district and within walking distance of the ballpark. *16554 N 83rd Av., Peoria; 623/773-2424;* **themoonsaloon.com**. You are also close to the interesting entertainment venues in the eastern part of Glendale, which we cover in our American Family Fields of Phoenix / Milwaukee Brewers chapter.

WHERE TO STAY

There is no hotel near the ballpark. The closest hotel is a Comfort Suites State Farm Stadium Arena near the 101 loop (*9824 W. Camelback Rd., Glendale; 623-271-9005;* **comfort-**

suites.com), over a mile away. The official White Sox hotel in 2024 was SpringHill Suites Glendale (*7370 North Zanjero Blvd., Glendale; 623/772-9200; marriott.com*), while the Dodgers did not designate an official hotel in 2024.

If you want to stay relatively close to the ballpark, there are clusters of hotels near the 101/I-10 interchange (Holiday Inn Express, Quality Inn, Hilton Garden Inn, etc.) and the Westgate Entertainment District (ranging from Hampton Inn and Staybridge Suites to Renaissance Phoenix Glendale Hotel & Spa). These are chain hotels at various price points, and there is an abundance of choices.

Within a short drive is a classic Valley of the Sun resort, the Wigwam Resort and Spa. Built on a former Goodyear cotton farm, the resort opened in 1929 with enough rooms for 24 guests. Over the years, the emphasis changed to golf and spa living, and in that time the area around the resort morphed from open country to suburbia. A part of that 1929 building is still in use as a reminder of the resort's past. *Wigwam Resort and Spa, 300 Wigwam Boulevard, Litchfield Park; 800/327-0396; wigwamarizona.com.*

SPRING-TRAINING HISTORY: CHICAGO WHITE SOX

The Chicago White Sox have held spring training in Excelsior Springs, Mo. (1901-1902); Mobile (1903); Marlin, Texas (1904); New Orleans (1905-1906); Mexico City (1907); Los Angeles (1908); San Francisco (1909-1910); Mineral Wells, Texas (1911, 1916-1919); Waco, Texas (1912, 1920); Paso Robles, Cal. (1913-1915); Waxahachie, Texas (1921); Seguin, Texas (1922-1923); Winter Haven, Fla. (1924); Shreveport, La. (1925-1928); Dallas (1929); San Antonio (1930-1932); Pasadena, Cal. (1933-1942, 1946-1950); French Lick, Ind. (1943-1944); Terre Haute, Ind. (1945); Palm Springs, Cal. (1951); El Centro, Cal. (1952-1953); Tampa (1954-1959); Sarasota (1960-1997); Tucson (1998-2010); and Glendale (2011-present).

SPRING-TRAINING HISTORY: LOS ANGELES DODGERS

The Los Angeles Dodgers have trained in the following locations: Charlotte, N.C. (1901); Columbia, S.C. (1902-1906); Jacksonville (1907-1909); Hot Springs, Ark. (1910-1912); Augusta, Ga. (1913-1914); Daytona Beach (1915-1916); Hot Springs, Ark. (1917-1918); Jacksonville (1919-1920); New Orleans (1921); Jacksonville (1922); Clearwater (1923-1932); Miami (1933); Orlando (1934-1935); Clearwater (1936-1940); Havana (1941-1942); Bear Mountain, N.Y. (1943-1945); Daytona Beach (1946); Havana (1947); Ciudad Trujillo, Dominican Republic (1948); Vero Beach (1949-2008); Phoenix (2008); and Glendale (2009-present).

REMEMBERING DODGERTOWN

It's impossible to write about Dodgers spring training and not discuss the team's longtime Florida home, Vero Beach's Dodgertown. Even though the Dodgers moved from the Grapefruit League to the Cactus League over 10 years ago, the topic of Dodgertown and its bucolic beauty is still a topic of discussion among spring-training aficionados.

With the Brooklyn (and then Los Angeles) Dodgers as a tenant, Dodgertown was one of the most historic venues in spring-training history. Walking through the grounds of Dodgertown was a timeless experience: you were likely to run into the likes of Tommy Lasorda or Sandy Koufax checking out the latest phenoms, while the ghosts of Don Drysdale and Walter Alston hung back in the shadows. The place didn't change much during in the 50 years the Dodgers were there—which was both a good thing and a bad thing.

The Dodgers were attracted to the area by Bud Holman, a local entrepreneur and director of Eastern Air Lines. He persuaded Buzzie Bavasi (then the farm director of the Brooklyn Dodgers) to consolidate spring training for the Dodgers and their 30-plus farm teams. The city of Vero Beach wasn't sure this was a good idea—as a matter of fact, the city refused to put in a swimming pool that Holman requested—so technically the Dodgers contracted with Holman, who in turn leased the land from the city.

The Dodgers were so pleased with spring training in Vero Beach that by 1952 the Dodgers signed a 21-year lease with the city for a true Dodgertown at a former Naval air base. As part of the lease, the Dodgers agreed that the entire major-league club and 50 percent of the Dodgers' farm teams would train in Vero Beach. The players were put up in former Naval barracks.

The Dodgers then furthered their commitment a few months later by investing $100,000 in a new ballpark, named Holman Stadium, with 1,500 steel chairs brought from Ebbets Field and the Polo Grounds. Holman Stadium has an impressive lineage: it was designed by Norman Bel Geddes (designer of the Futurama building at the 1964 New York World's Fair and the creative genius behind a proposed domed stadium for the Dodgers that, alas, was never built) and engineered by Captain Emil Praeger, whose firm (Praeger-Kavanagh-Waterbury) also engineered Dodger Stadium in Los Angeles and Shea Stadium in New York City.

In the end, the needs of the Los Angeles Dodgers were different than the needs of the Brooklyn Dodgers. Even when the team moved to Los Angeles, Brooklyn fans made the familiar trip to Dodgertown. But as these fans died out, they weren't replaced by Los Angelinos, and crowds shrunk for spring training. The Dodgers attempted to shift spring training to Arizona several times before successfully working out a Camelback Ranch deal, and despite the many fond memories of training in Florida, it made sense for the Los Angeles Dodgers to take up spring residence closer to the team's fan base.

Today, Dodgertown is called Jackie Robinson Training Complex and is used by sporting teams of all kinds, including youth tournaments of all sorts. It's now run by Major League Baseball and has enjoyed new popularity with the resurgence of sports tourism. *Jackie Robinson Training Complex, 3901 26th St., Vero Beach; 866/656-4900;* **mlb.com/robinson-training-complex**.

GOODYEAR BALLPARK / CINCINNATI REDS / CLEVELAND GUARDIANS

QUICK FACTS

- **Capacity**: 10,311
- **Year Opened**: 2009
- **Dimensions**: 345L, 380LC, 410C, 380RC, 345R
- **Dugout Locations**: Reds on the third-base side, Guardians on the first-base side
- **Practice Times**: Gates open at 9 a.m., with practices starting at 9:30 a.m.
- **Gates Open**: 90 minutes before game time. Home batting practice, 10:15-11:15 a.m. at complex; visitors batting practice, 11:15 a.m.-12:15 p.m.; visitors infield, 12:15-12:25 p.m. Add five hours for a night (6:05 p.m.) game.
- **Ticket Lines**: 800/745-3000, 866/488-7423 (Guardians), 623/882-3130 (Reds)
- **Address**: 1933 S. Ballpark Way, Goodyear, AZ 85338
- **Directions**: From Downtown Phoenix/East Valley: West on I-10 to Exit 127, Bullard Avenue and proceed south (left off exit). Bullard Avenue will

turn into West Lower Buckeye Road. Stay to the right and turn right on to Wood Boulevard. From West Phoenix/Surface streets route: South on Litchfield Road to Van Buren. West on Van Buren to Bullard Avenue. South on Bullard Avenue, which will become West Lower Buckeye Road. Stay to the right and turn right on to Wood Boulevard.

A LITTLE BIT OF OHIO IN THE DESERT

When the Cleveland Indians returned in 2009 for a second stint in the Arizona League, it was a return to roots. The Indians and the New York Giants comprised the beginnings of the modern-day Cactus League, so to speak, when Bill Veeck wanted spring operations closer to his ranch in the Tucson area and made arrangements accordingly for the 1947 season.

And when the Cincinnati Reds arrived in 2010, it made for a unique all-Ohio training complex. There's no other two-team training complex where the two teams are from the same state. Geography usually breeds competitive juices; one can't imagine the Dodgers and Angels sharing a complex, or the Mets and Yankees sharing facilities. But it works here, where Ohio roots run deep.

There are plenty of ties between Ohio, Goodyear, and Goodyear Ballpark aside from baseball. In 1917, the Goodyear Tire and Rubber Company, still headquartered in Ohio, purchased 16,000 acres of land that make up part of modern Goodyear. It was an agricultural investment: the land was used to grow cotton, and Goodyear used that cotton to make airplane tires during World War I.

The land was chiefly agricultural and rural, but in 1946 the town of Goodyear was incorporated, complete with 151 homes and a grocery store. World War II provided a financial lift to the city after the Litchfield Naval Air Facility and the Goodyear Aircraft Corporation were located there, with blimps and Navy Blue Angels the order of the day. The facility ended up being converted to Phoenix Goodyear Airport, located directly east of the ballpark. It's still used as a freight airport and a storage area for grounded planes, easily seen from the upper floors of the grandstand.

When Goodyear Ballpark was first presented to city officials, it was envisioned as the centerpiece of a larger downtown-style complex that included retail, office space, and hotels. But the economic turndown caused problems for the developer, and as a result the associated development did not take place. That's why there's so much open land next to the ballpark; the downtown-style development was envisioned both south and north of the ballpark.

There has been plenty of growth in the area—lots of housing has been built west and south of the ballpark—but in terms of retail and entertainment, all the growth has come north of the ballpark, closer to I-10. In general, Goodyear has been one of the fastest-growing communities in all of Arizona, not just the Phoenix area. The issue: without enough people in the ballpark area generating economic activity, no developer wanted to make an investment. Now, however, city officials say they are seeing investments in a growing part of the Valley, and we should see the long-awaited development in the next few years.

INSIDER'S TIP

Some of that development has already started: drive by the Reds and Guardians training complexes and you'll see the new multifamily developments that went up in 2023-2024. Coming up—possibly in time for spring training 2026—is a new $25-million development north of the ballpark at Estrella Parkway and Yuma Road. The final tenant mix still needs to be determined, but expect the likes of Starbucks and fast-casual dining. Also expected in the same area: a new indoor family entertainment center.

In the end Goodyear Ballpark is a nice, simple facility with a unique industrial finish. The training facilities for the Guardians and Reds sit south of the ballpark on South Wood Boulevard and represent state-of-the-art spring training and rehab facilities.

INSIDER'S TIP

If you're heading to practice fields and not the main ballpark, you'll want to plug some slightly different addresses into the GPS. The Guardians workout

facility is located at 2601 S. Wood Boulevard, while the
Reds training facility is at 3125 S. Wood Boulevard.
Each training complex has six full practice fields and
two half fields. The two fields to the north of each
complex are designated for use solely by the teams; the
four cloverleaf fields are at the disposal of Goodyear
for youth and adult baseball.

There are some unique touches to the ballpark. First,
smaller clubhouses are located in a building past right field
topped by the Right Field Pavilion concessions area. Players
enter the ballpark from right-field doors. Because the
workout facilities are so close, the teams prep for games at
those facilities (including batting practice) and then arrive at
the ballpark ready to play. As we noted, the finishes
throughout—ranging from the grandstand to the outfield
building and concession booths—are consistent, accented
with an industrial motif.

History is represented at the ballpark. An exhibit from the
Play Ball Experience, devoted to Cactus League history, can
be found in the entry area, across from the Team Store. Given
that the Indians were there at the beginning of the Cactus
League, there is plenty of history to recount, with the displays
providing nice windows both on the team's past and the local
history. Right inside the home-plate gates you'll find the Ohio
Cup, awarded to the team that wins the annual interleague
series between the teams.

INSIDER'S TIP
No matter where you park, enter the ballpark through
the home-plate gate. You'll get a good look at the baseball sculpture, The Ziz, from noted artist Donald
Lipski. Measuring 60 feet, 6 inches, the 6,000-point
sculpture combines some baseball elements (baseball

seams) into a stylized and striking focal point for the ballpark. It cost the city of Goodyear $450,000.

INSIDER'S TIP
One thing that distinguishes the Goodyear Ballpark game-day experience: live organ music, which is somewhat of an endangered species in any spring-training ballpark.

INSIDER'S TIP
American and Frontier offer daily direct service from Cincinnati or Cleveland to Phoenix. Allegiant runs limited service from Cincinnati to Phoenix-Mesa Gateway Airport.

Things are run in Goodyear pretty much the way the Guardians and Reds ran things in Florida: low-key, with an emphasis on the game. (Although Goodyear Ballpark is also notable for something else: its own mascot, Zizzy.) The remote location may scare some spring-training fans from making the trip to Goodyear, but don't be deterred: Goodyear Ballpark is an underrated facility and worth the drive. The general area around the ballpark is a mix of planned communities (to the west), agricultural land (to the north), the airport and Avondale (to the east), and Estrella Mountain to the south. But with new services and hotels opening annually in the Goodyear area, a Goodyear Ballpark run is increasingly convenient.

INSIDER'S TIP
We can't walk the Goodyear Ballpark concourse without remembering Indians Hall of Famer Bob Feller, who traditionally set up a table by the ballpark front entrance—wherever the Indians were training—

and sold autographs. He also threw out the first pitch here. His presence is felt years after his death.

THE SPRING-TRAINING BALLPARK EXPERIENCE

CONCESSIONS

Each year sees a new wave of concessions at Goodyear Ballpark, with the city working to introduce a new set of food and drink offerings. As a result, Goodyear Ballpark has become somewhat of a foodie paradise in the Cactus League, so definitely go to the ballpark hungry. In the past we saw new food offerings like loaded corn-dog nuggets, garlic Parmesan waffle fries, and the ultimate indulgence: The Cheesy Changeup, two grilled-cheese sandwiches cradling a half-pound cheeseburger.

Recommended if still offered: a green-chile burger (highly recommended) and a green chili-infused chicken sausage. Likely still available: garlic fries, Funnel Cake fries, and a Philly cheesesteak/hot dog combo. And, as always, you can find a wide variety of hot dogs, top-notch brats, burgers, freshly prepared French fries, and other ballpark fare at the general food stands, but we'd recommend heading to the specialty stands for something unique.

INSIDER'S TIP
Yes, Cincinnati fans, there is Skyline Chili for your hot dogs. Find it at the Hangar 46 stand and the Queen City Grill. Yes, Cleveland fans, there is Bertman Ball Park Mustard at most condiment stations. And yes, you can find a Cleveland Polish Boy at the 1901 Charter Grille.

There's also a separate Philly cheesesteak stand behind home plate worth a stop, and a Baskin-Robbins ice-cream stand down the first-base line. Other specialty booths feature barbeque, fry bread, smokies, and a taquito dog, a hot dog wrapped in cheese and a tortilla, deep fried and topped with guacamole, sour cream, and pico de gallo. And, as you'll find in many spring-training ballparks, the food offerings are spiced up with the presence of food trucks.

One other notable offering: an expansion of beer selections. Most are of the MillerCoors variety, along with some indies and import offerings like Four Peaks, Pabst Blue Ribbon (in the obligatory tallboy), and Heineken. A local favorite, SanTan Devil's Ale, is on tap as well. In 2019, Goodyear Ballpark unveiled a shaded Arizona Craft Beer Corner down the third-base line, offering microbrews from Arizona.

INSIDER'S TIP
If still offered, come early for the Happy Hour, which features discounted beers and hot dogs.

INSIDER'S TIP
You can bring in a single unopened water bottle and unopened snacks (chips, peanuts, etc.). You cannot bring in prepared food in your own container.

AUTOGRAPHS

Generally speaking, this is a mixed place to snare an autograph. There's no dedicated or traditional signing spot, and with the players entering and leaving from a right-field clubhouse (both teams dress in their nearby training complexes), there's little chance for anyone to stop and sign in the midst of a game. Your best chance for an autograph is to hope a player will come out to sign at some point down the line.

PARKING

Free. When a big crowd is expected, ballpark officials will send out carts to help those with physical challenges more easily reach the front gates. There is limited street parking in the area, but you'll find it to be quite a hike from these spots to the ballpark. One tip: The ballpark is close enough to the training complexes that you can park on Wood Boulevard, hit the morning practices, and then walk over for the 1:05 p.m. game.

> **INSIDER'S TIP**
> People sometimes complain that parking is on a grassy field and not a paved parking lot. But most folks don't realize that for the remaining 10 months of the year we're not talking about a parking lot: we are talking about youth soccer fields. And those soccer fields play a vital role in year-round youth activities.

FOR THE KIDS

The Kids Zone is located in the right-field corner and features standard ballpark inflatable games, such as a bouncy house. In addition, there's a small Wiffle-ball diamond—complete with smaller backstop—for the kids within the ballpark fence. For the older kids—i.e., millennials—there are a number of games located down the left-field line, including corn hole and rock climbing.

WHERE TO SIT

There are no bleachers in the ballpark—only 8,007 theater-style seats. And they're mostly pretty good, except for a few clunkers. For instance, stay away from Section 105: you'll be sitting in back of a distracting tarp.

INSIDER'S TIP

Section numbering begins with 101 in the left-field corner and runs through 123 in the right-field corner. The concourse is in the back of the seating area, so no aisle runs through the seating bowl.

INSIDER'S TIP
To sit near the Reds dugout on the third-base side, buy a ticket in Sections 106-110. To sit near the Guardians dugout on the first-base side, buy a ticket in Sections 114-118.

The berm isn't as large as found in other spring ballparks: it seats only 1,530, and we find it's rarely crowded. Maybe it's because there's only a little bit of prime berm area: the bullpens are beyond the home-run fence (Guardians to the left, Reds to the right) and occupy areas that normally would be swarmed by fans. Similarly, the Right Field Pavilion and clubhouse takes up a lot of prime space in right field from the power alley to the foul pole. And there's one big disadvantage to sitting on the berm: you can't see the scoreboard.

If you seek shade, go for Sections 110-114, as they're protected from the sun by the press box and suites, which are built up high. The Right Field Pavilion has plenty of shaded bar and couch seating, as well as its own bar. Better yet, go for a ticket in the Club area (106A, 106B, 107A): the seats are totally shaded and feature padded seats. Like many spring-training ballparks, there is free sunscreen, with dispensers next to the restrooms.

The right-field pavilion has a bar with eight tap handles, lounge furniture, and nine big-screen TVs. Fans may purchase group tickets that include the buffet, or just mingle on the top level if they have seats elsewhere and no group has reserved the entire pavilion. Unlike most spring-training ballparks, Goodyear Ballpark offers half-price tickets for kids ages 3-12 in the outfield box, outfield reserved, and berm seating sections.

The rooftop Terrace ticket is pricier than most tickets in Goodyear Ballpark ($19; food extra), but so worth it: you can see for miles, and your views of the game are framed by Estrella Mountain to the south and the White Tank Mountains to the northwest. There are concessions within, so you won't need to leave to snare a beer and a dog. The risk: tickets to the Terrace are sold only on game day, and they do sell out quickly.

INSIDER'S TIP

Head to the center-field pub patio for some beer and shade. You can sit there if you buy a cheap berm ticket. (Or any ticket, for that matter; it's open seating.) You won't be able to see the scoreboard, but then again, on a warmer late-March day, you'll appreciate the shade more.

SELFIE SPOT

The aforementioned Ziz sculpture outside the ballpark is by far the best spot for a selfie at Goodyear Ballpark.

WHAT TO DO OUTSIDE THE BALLPARK

The southwest corner of Phoenix—especially the communities along I-10, including Goodyear and Avondale—tend to be dominated by planned communities, big-box retailers, and plenty of chain developments. Not that there's anything wrong with that, but you don't travel hundreds of miles to do what you can do at home.

So your choice is simple: stay in the area and make the best of things, or hunker down in Phoenix or a more centrally located area and drive out to games.

Sticking around is actually made easier these days by the general growth in the area, particularly north of the freeway. There are two sports bars worth your attention, as well as other attractions.

Augie's Sports Grill is a good destination during March Madness, with multiple TV screens providing the action. The food is strictly pub grub, but the drinks are cheap (particularly during Happy Hour, which runs daily through 7 p.m.). *Augie's Sports Grill, 15605 W. Roosevelt St., Goodyear; 623/932-0001;* ***augiessportsgrillgoodyear.com.***

It's not technically a sports bar, but it is an oasis: Roman's Oasis is a sprawling cowboy hangout, featuring live weekend music (Southern rock, of course), karaoke, decent food (tots!), and plenty of bar space. Leave the credit cards at home: cash only. *Roman's Oasis, 16825 W. Yuma Rd., Goodyear; 623/932-0922.*

Though we recommend coming hungry to the ballpark, we know many of you simply will not spend much money on food at the ballpark; the biggest complaint we hear from fans is that food is too expensive. Fair enough. If you want to grab a bite before you head to the ballpark, there is an abundance of fast-food joints on the I-10 strip north of the ballpark. If you think you can handle a big lunch before heading to the ballpark, we'd recommend Rudy's BBQ (*45 N. Litchfield Rd., Goodyear; 480/663-6311, rudysbbq.com*), a Texas-based chain with an outpost on the south side of I-10 and right on the way to Goodyear Ballpark. It features all the basic smoked meats —brisket, ribs, pulled pork, and barbecued chicken—along with the expected Southern sides.

The Phoenix brewpub scene has definitely arrived in the West Valley, and in Goodyear you are close to one of the good ones, Saddle Mountain Brewing Company (*15651 W. Roosevelt St., Goodyear; 623/249-5520; saddlemountainbrewing.com*), just up Estrella Parkway from the ballpark. There is an aviation theme to the beers and décor. There's both indoor and outdoor seating, perfect for a post-game snort. Get there early on a Friday or Saturday if you want a table.

A little farther afield, but also worth the drive, is 8-Bit Aleworks (*1050 Fairway Dr., Building F, Suite 101, Avondale; 623/925-1650; 8-bitaleworks.com*). This microbrewery features a 46-seat tasting room, with a wide range of beers on tap. The brewery's name is a reference to what many consider to be the first golden era of video games: 8-bit arcade games like Donkey Kong Jr. Yes, the tasting room features old-school gaming consoles.

For food as opposed to a beer in a bar, one of our favorite spots in the whole Valley is the Angry Crab Shack (*310 N. Litchfield Rd., Goodyear; 480/878-6900; angrycrabshack.com*). Yes, we love the notion of an abundance of seafood in the middle of the desert, which makes Angry Crab Shack even more of an oasis. Most folks will select their seafood by the pound, choose a sauce and heat level, put on a bib, and go to town. For those wanting something a little less audacious than a bag full of seafood, there are plenty of worthy menu options—po' boys, fried frog legs, fried cod, and so on. Angry Crab Shack can get pretty busy at dinner, so plan to wait at the bar.

There's been plenty of other development in the West Valley worth your attention if you head out to a Reds or Guardians spring-training game. In our Camelback Ranch–Glendale chapter we discuss the Westgate Entertainment District, anchored by Desert Diamond Arena and sporting plenty of restaurant, bar, and entertainment options. In our Peoria chapter we discuss the Peoria P83 entertainment district, surrounding Peoria Stadium. Both of these areas are an easy drive up the 101 from Goodyear Ballpark.

WHERE TO STAY

There are no hotels within walking distance of the ballpark, but there are plenty as you get close to I-10. The official hotel for the Reds in 2024 was the Marriott Residence Inn (*7350 N. Zanjero Blvd., Glendale; 623/772-8900; marriott.com*). The Guardians do not designate an official hotel. Other hotels within a close drive include Hampton Inn and Suites (*2000 N. Litchfield Rd., Goodyear; 623/536-1313; hilton.com*), Springhill Suites (*1370 N. Bullard Av., Goodyear; 602/354-9540; marriott.com*), Holiday Inn Express (*1313 N. Litchfield Rd., Goodyear; 623/535-1313; ihg.com*), TownPlace Suites (*13971 W. Celebrate Life Way, Goodyear; 623/535-5009; marriott.com*), Residence Inn by Marriott (*2020 N. Litchfield Rd., Goodyear; 623/866-1313; marriott.com*), Quality Inn & Suites (*950 N. Dysart, Glendale; 623/932-9191; choicehotels.com*), Holiday Inn & Suites (*1188 N. Dysart Rd., Goodyear; 623/547-1313; ihg.com*), Tru by Hilton (*1430 N. Bullard Av., Goodyear; 602/354-9530; hilton.com*), and Comfort Suites (*15575 W. Roosevelt St., Goodyear; 520/257-3134; choicehotels.com*).

These hotels are relatively close to the ballpark, to the north on the I-10 strip.

If you choose to stay in Goodyear in a more upscale venue, check out the Wigwam Golf Resort (*300 E. Wigwam*

Blvd., Litchfield Park, 623/935-3811; wigwamarizona.com), a 400-acre, 331-room complex with three 18-hole championship courses. The resort dates back to 1918 as lodging for ranch suppliers and as a resort to 1929, but has been seriously upgraded in recent years. The Wigwam Bar, with its indoor/outdoor seating, is definitely a draw. It's part of the first ranch building, Organization House, with the original 1918 fireplace.

SPRING-TRAINING HISTORY: CINCINNATI REDS

The Cincinnati Reds have trained in the following locations: Cincinnati (1901-1902); Augusta, Ga. (1903); Dallas (1904); Jacksonville (1905); San Antonio (1906); Marlin Springs, Texas (1907); St. Augustine (1908); Atlanta (1909); Hot Springs, Ark. (1910-1911); Columbus, Ga. (1912); Mobile, Ala. (1913); Alexandria, La. (1914-1915); Shreveport (1916-1917); Montgomery, Ala. (1918); Waxahachie, Texas (1919); Miami (1920); Cisco, Texas (1921); Mineral Wells, Texas (1922); Orlando (1923-1930); Tampa (1931-1942); Bloomington, Ind. (1943-1945); Tampa (1946-1987); Plant City, Fla. (1988-1997); Sarasota (1998-2009); and Goodyear (2010-present).

The ballparks used by the Reds in Sarasota (Ed Smith Stadium) and Plant City (Plant City Stadium) still stand. Ed Smith Stadium has been renovated and is now spring home of the Baltimore Orioles.

SPRING-TRAINING HISTORY: CLEVELAND GUARDIANS

The Cleveland Guardians have trained in the following locations: Cleveland (1901); New Orleans (1902-1903); San Antonio (1904); Atlanta (1905-1906); Macon, Ga. (1907-1908); Mobile, Ala. (1909); Alexandria, La. (1910-1911); Mobile, Ala. (1912); Pensacola, Fla. (1913); Athens, Ga. (1914); San Antonio

(1915); New Orleans (1916-1920); Dallas (1921-1922); Lakeland (1923-1927); New Orleans (1928-1939); Ft. Myers (1940-1941); Clearwater (1942); Lafayette, Ind. (1943-1945); Clearwater (1946); Tucson (1947-1992); Winter Haven (1993-2008); Goodyear (2009-present). Some of these former spring homes still stand, such as Henley Field in Lakeland and Hi Corbett Field in Tucson.

Demolished in 2024: Chain of Lakes Park in Winter Haven. The Cleveland Indians were the last spring-training tenant of this modest ballpark, which had been used for college and high-school ball since the departure of the Tribe to Arizona. The site will still be used for baseball in the form of youth tournaments.

HOHOKAM STADIUM / THE ATHLETICS

QUICK FACTS

- **Capacity**: 10,000
- **Year Opened**: 1997; renovated 2015
- **Dimensions**: 340L, 385LC, 411C, 385RC, 350R
- **Dugout Location**: First-base side
- **Practice Times**: Practices begin at 10 a.m. at Lew Wolff Training Complex at Fitch Park (651 N. Center, Mesa)
- **Gates Open**: Grandstand opens two hours before game time. Athletics batting practice, until 11 a.m.; visitors batting practice, 11 a.m.-noon.
- **Ticket Line**: 877/493-2255
- **Address**: 1235 N. Center St., Mesa 85201
- **Directions**: From Phoenix, take 202 Loop east to Exit 12 (McKellips Road), turn right on W. McKellips Road; and turn right onto N. Center Street. Hohokam Stadium will be on the left-hand side of the street.

PUTTING DOWN ROOTS IN MESA

With the move of the A's from Oakland to Sacramento—temporarily, anyway—there will be a lot of change for the team to absorb in 2025. Luckily, the Athletics on the field won't need to confront that change until the regular season, as the team plans to spend spring training at Hohokam Stadium and the Lew Wolff Training Complex, with the team embarking on a second decade in Mesa.

Whether the fans follow, however, will be an interesting question. In Mesa, the A's became a solid draw, with Oakland fans making the trip to Mesa in increasingly larger numbers every spring. Will Oakland fans continue the Arizona pilgrimage? Will they be replaced by Sacramento fans? It will be a fascinating spring at Hohokam Stadium.

INSIDER'S TIP

While the team plays the 2025-2027 seasons in Sacramento before a planned Las Vegas move, the franchise will play as the Athletics or the A's, with no geographic designation. The team will share a ballpark with the Sacramento River Cats, with the River Cats retaining the geographic designation.

It took several years and several stops to get to this point. Previously the A's trained at the first version of Hohokam Stadium, which opened in 1977, but the Athletics soon bailed for Scottsdale Stadium. Hohokam was rebuilt in 1997 for the Chicago Cubs, and then upgraded yet again for the 2015 arrival of the Athletics. (It opened as Hohokam Park per a concourse plaque, but somehow acquired the Hohokam Stadium name upon the arrival of the Athletics. Confusingly, the 2024 MLB spring-training media guide referred both to

Hohokam Park and Hohokam Stadium.) Every trace of the Cubbie red and blue was removed from Hohokam Stadium, as the A's and Mesa forged a new identity.

Mesa and the Athletics made some serious decisions about Hohokam Stadium a decade ago that, seen today, were great choices. First, a layer of green-and-gold paint—as well as lots of grey—replaced the Cubs red and blue, giving the place a consistent look. Second, the ballpark was downsized to a capacity of 10,000, from the 12,575-fan capacity when the Cubs were in town. Some poorly situated seating was removed to make way for party decks, complete with their own concessions, picnic tables, and drink rails. While these drink rails are a little too far off the action to view much of the game, they still attract plenty of fans. Perhaps the best thing about both party decks: they are shaded. Third, the A's and Mesa installed what was then the largest videoboard in all of spring training, providing crystal-clear replays, player shots, and more to A's fans. The high-def videoboard is bright and clearly visible from every part of the ballpark—except for the folks sitting on the berm in the left-field corner. (So, don't sit there!) For players, an expanded clubhouse with new weight room provides more comfort than experienced at Phoenix Municipal Stadium. And then there's the Lew Wolff Training Center at Fitch Park, which raises Athletics training abilities to a new level.

INSIDER'S TIP

The Athletics do not work out at Hohokam Stadium during the practice portion of training camp, before games begin. Instead, the Athletics practice at Lew Wolff Training Center at Fitch Park (651 N. Center St., Mesa), just up the road from Hohokam Stadium. Practices begin at 10 a.m., with the major-league squad dressing at Hohokam Stadium and then transported down to Fitch Park. Access to players at Fitch Park is decent, as fans are directed to seating and standing-room areas in the middle of the cloverleaf training fields.

There are four fields at Fitch Park, and they're all used in spring training. They also feature bleacher seating, as well as a concession stand.

An Athletics spring-training game is a quintessential Cactus League experience. The team is a solid draw, and the ballpark is a significant upgrade over the team's former spring home. Plenty of parking means there is plenty of tail-gating before a game, and that atmosphere carries in the ball-park. The Athletics have made Hohokam Stadium their own, making a visit worth your time.

THE SPRING-TRAINING BALLPARK EXPERIENCE

CONCESSIONS

Overall, the food at Hohokam Stadium is middling, so come with a game plan. With the ballpark sporting a 1970s design, most concession stands—cashless, of course—are located under the grandstand, in a concourse with no view of the action. So you'll need to plan your food runs to minimize your time away from the game action. We will likely still see some Oakland touches to the proceedings—the popular Ike's Love & Sandwiches, an Oakland institution with several Valley outposts, attracts some long lines—but we'll see whether hot dogs pitched as Oakland favorites are offered. (The Oakland Dog, with mac and cheese, chilies and bacon, was especially tasty.) If you're looking for something a little offbeat, try the organic pizza from Freak Brothers Pizza, deli sandwiches (hot sliced pastrami and corned beef on challah bread from local fave Chompie's; see our Los Angeles Angels chapter for more on Chompie's), or the short-rib tacos from Gadzooks Tacos. And, of course, there's the ubiquitous noodle stand, popular as ever.

One food item is a particular favorite: the foot-long corn dog, located at a stand in a cluster of concessions off third base. If this particular concessionaire returns in 2025—and we hope they do—head there and have one of the best food items in the Cactus League.

A great selection of beers both local and national can be found at various stands throughout the ballpark, including offerings from local stars Four Peaks and national stars Lagunitas Brewing Company and Goose Island. And while the best beer stands are not hard to find—they are in the two party decks down each line—they are not necessarily emphasized, either. Beware: there were no beers on tap in the main concourse in 2024.

The food lineup can be a little fluid: the A's brought in food trucks to augment traditional concessions, so there was usually a surprise or two in the food lineup.

While every Cactus League ballpark has a team store—or two or three—Hohokam Stadium in the past has featured a Baseballism shop, with unique lines of baseball-centric and design-oriented T-shirts and sweatshirts. Baseballism can be found in both in permanent shops (like the one in The Battery, next to Atlanta's Truist Park, as well as the storefront in downtown Scottsdale) and pop-ups. Worth a visit.

AUTOGRAPHS

Players usually hang out before the game in front of the tarp next to the home dugout down the first-base line. You can also hang around Fitch Park and hit morning practices, which begin at 9:30 a.m. Otherwise, it's hard to snare an autograph at Hohokam Stadium.

PARKING

There is adequate paid parking next to the ballpark: 3,000 spots, give or take. The cost is a reasonable $5. When the A's first moved to Hohokam Stadium, there was a noticeable dropoff in tailgating from the Cubs days; those Chicago fans know how to party out of their car trunks. In recent years we've noticed more tailgating at Hohokam Stadium.

Many fans drive into the surrounding neighborhood to park for free or with a homeowner. These spots go for $5 or so. In addition, ballpark street parking is prohibited in the neighborhood surrounding Hohokam Stadium. Beware: Mesa law authorities rigorously enforce the signs warning against ballgame parking. We feel $5 is a pretty reasonable parking fee, as you'll be walking several blocks on what can be a very hot day to get to and from the ballpark for a free spot. But some folks will still make the long march to snare free parking.

Getting into the ballpark is no great shakes: there are long lines if you're coming from the north on Center Street. Our advice is to loop to the south of the ballpark and make your way north on Center Street. You may also snare some free street parking if you arrive early enough. One spot where the parking is free: Brown Road, south of the ballpark, where you'll find crowds parking for free and walking the short distance to Hohokam Stadium.

INSIDER'S TIP

Hohokam Stadium is less than two miles from downtown Mesa. You'll find folks who park downtown and then make the 40-minute walk to the ballpark. On a hot day, this can certainly be a chore; it's not the walk to the ballpark that will knock you out, it's the walk back after spending three hours at a ballpark. Be warned that most downtown parking in Mesa carries a fee, but on weekends and after 5 p.m. the downtown lots are free.

WHERE TO SIT

There's an abundance of shade at Hohokam Stadium, thanks to a canopy covering much of the grandstand. That means a very large share of the 200-level seating—basically, anything from Section 202 on the third-base side down to Section 213— is now fully shaded at the start of the game. (If you sit in the closer 100-level seats, you'll be in the sun. Bring sunscreen, as there are no sunscreen dispensers as found in other spring-training ballparks.) There's also shade in the upper-level group picnic areas.

If your only choice is between seats far down the line or the berm, go for the berm, still one of the great areas in spring training. It's easily accessible via a center-field entrance (close to much of the parking), it has its own concessions, and it's still the venue for hardcore fans. A warning: The berm can be a serious sun field on a hot day (in other words, apply your sunscreen before leaving your car or bring it in a tube—no spray cans allowed in the ballpark).

INSIDER'S TIP
Hohokam Stadium seat numbers follow the even/odd convention: even numbers to the left of home plate and odd numbers to the right. When you have a choice, sit in an odd-numbered section.

INSIDER'S TIP
If you get to the berm early, stake out a spot in right field. Both bullpens are located there beyond the home-run fence, and fans can sit right next to the pens. The A's bullpen is closest to the playing field.

INSIDER'S TIP
Sit in an even-numbered seat if you want a great back-drop—the Superstition Mountains—to the action.

INSIDER'S TIP
The Hyatt Place Patio is a reserved covered area above Terrace Box sections 210/212 for guests to enjoy a catered meal and a game.

FOR THE KIDS

There's a small kids' activity area in dead-center field, the Stomper Kid Zone, with plenty of diversions for the youngsters. In general, the berm is nirvana for families, with plenty of kids playing and running around during the course of a game and crowding the bullpens.

SELFIE SPOT

Your best bet: a portable Hohokam Stadium sign, set up in the outfield concourse.

IF YOU GO

WHERE TO STAY

Mesa does feel like it is a separate area of the Phoenix region, and if you're a true A's fan you'll want to spend as much time as possible hanging around the ballpark and practice facility. There are a number of hotels within two miles of the ballpark:

- Delta Hotels by Marriott, 200 N. Centennial Way, Mesa; 480/898-8300; *marriott.com*. Technically, this is the hotel closest to the ballpark, a little over a mile away.
- The Azure Hotel, 651 E. Main St., Mesa; 480/621-6375; *theazurehotel.com*. A renovated Baymont Inn, this is a boutique hotel with an old motor court vibe in the middle of downtown Mesa.
- Hyatt Place Phoenix/Mesa, W. Bass Pro Dr., Mesa; 480/969-8200; *hyatt.com*. This hotel is also close to

Sloan Park, home of the Cubs, making it a good central base for spring training.

The official team hotel in 2024 was the Doubletree Suites Hotel (*320 N. 44th St., Phoenix; 602/225-0500; hilton.com*).

RV RESORTS NEAR THE BALLPARK

The ballpark is in the western part of Mesa, putting it a decent distance from the many RV parks in eastern Mesa and Apache Junction.

And there is an abundance of them, to be sure. Mesa is known in some circles as being the RV park center of the Phoenix area. That's not necessarily a bad thing. There are at least 16 RV parks in the greater Mesa area, and that's not counting more in Tempe, Gilbert, Chandler, and Apache Junction. Check out the likes of Towerpoint or Good Life (*cal-am.com*), and the highly recommended Mesa Spirit (*mesaspirit.com*), but be warned that in general the RV resorts in Mesa are really snowbird camps.

NEARBY RESTAURANTS AND BREWPUBS

Mesa has developed into a foodie destination featuring both long-time favorites and hipster haunts with eclectic offerings. Take, for example, downtown's Espiritu Cocktails + Comida (*123 W. Main St., Mesa; 480/272-6825; espiritumesa.com*), billed as a Mexican cocktail lounge. But it's more more than that, as chef and owner Roberto Centeno is a James Beard Award semifinalist and the menu features the elevated likes of birria dumplings and *papancha*. If you're not feeling elevated, there are shots and oysters on the menu as well.

Mesa also features the Tipsy Chicken, where Korean fried chicken dominates the menu. Korean fried chicken is sloppy and delicious bar food, and you're missing out if you've never tried it. *Tipsy Chicken, 1933 W. Main St., Suite 7, Mesa; 480-265-8766;* **tipsychickenaz.com.**

A Mexican mainstay in the general area is Serrano's Mexican Food, with several locations throughout the Valley. The Serrano family has been in business in Arizona since 1919, but at that time the family business was clothing. In 1979 the Serrano family ditched the clothing and shifted into the Mexican restaurant business, keeping the Serrano logo. You'll find the usual Mexican fare at Serrano's, though there's a noted emphasis on seafood dishes like *pescado a la tortilla* (tilapia encrusted with tortilla) and *enchiladas de camaron* (shrimp enchiladas). *Serrano's Fine Mexican Food, 1964 E. McKellips Rd., Mesa; 480/649-3503;* **serranosaz.com.**

Worth a short drive is the Blue Adobe, which features New Mexico cuisine, as opposed to the Southwest cuisine found everywhere else in the Valley. This is New Mexico comfort food. *Blue Adobe Grille, 144 N. Country Club Dr., Mesa; 480/962-1000;* **originalblueadobe.com.**

The ballpark is north of downtown Mesa. While other communities in the Valley of the Sun are forced to create downtowns from scratch, Mesa has a historic one. And if the bustle found in some areas of the Valley grates on your nerves—yeah, we're looking at you, Scottsdale and downtown Tempe—some time spent in downtown Mesa will be a welcome remedy. For starters, downtown Mesa has its own historic districts and attractions; you could do worse than spending some time driving around and taking in a show or exhibit at the Mesa Arts Center (*1 E. Main St., Mesa; 480/644-6500;* **mesaartscenter.com**).

The Mesa Historical Museum (*Old Lehi School, 2345 N. Horne, Mesa; 480/835-2286;* **mesahistoricalmuseum.com**) works with the Cactus League on *Play Ball: The Arizona Spring Training Experience and Cactus League Hall of Fame* exhibit. The

2024 inductees included Ron Santo, Don Carson, and Bruce Bochy. *Adults $7; seniors and military, $5; youth (6-17), $5. Open Tuesday-Saturday, noon-4 p.m.*

In recent years, downtown Mesa has developed into a hipster hangout when compared to the rest of the Valley. You can view that hipster attitude in downtown Mesa at a great brewpub located in a 1900s-era adobe: Oro Brewing. Oro Brewing traditionally offers its own spring-training brews, as well as a slew of microbrews created in partnership with other area microbreweries. *Oro Brewing Co., 210 W. Main St., Mesa; 480/398-8247;* **orobrewing.com.**

As long as you're downtown, an impromptu beer crawl may be in order, with all the establishments located on Main Street. Stroll down to 12 West Brewing (*12 W. Main St., Mesa; 480/508-7018;* **12westbrewing.com**), Phantom Fox Beer Co. (*150 W. Main St., Mesa*), B.R.I. Taproom (*213 W. Main St., Mesa;* **thebeerresearchinstitute.com**), Pedal Haus Brewery (*201 W. Main St., Mesa;* **pedalhausbrewery.com**), and Chupacabra Taproom (*14 N. Robson, Mesa; 480/751-5566;* **chupacabratap room.com**).

We imagine there is a good number of day drinkers in the A's fanbase. There is also a good number of day drinkers in the Mesa area. If you're not acquainted with Mesa, day drinking is definitely a thing, as you'll find bars offering 6 a.m. Happy Hours. One such bar: The Hambone (*903 E. Main St.*), a renowned local dive bar that opens at 6 a.m. with drink specials and closes at 2 a.m. You go to The Hambone to drink, smoke, and watch sports.

SPRING-TRAINING HISTORY: THE ATHLETICS

Athletics spring-training sites have included: Philadelphia (1901, 1919); Charlotte, N.C. (1902); Jacksonville (1903, 1914-1918); Spartanburg, S.C. (1904); Shreveport (1905); Montgomery, Ala. (1906, 1923-1924); Dallas (1907); New Orleans (1908-1909); Atlanta (1910); San Antonio (1912-1913); Lake Charles, La. (1920-1921, 1938-1939); Eagle Pass, Texas (1922); Ft. Myers (1925-1936); Mexico City (1937); Anaheim, Cal. (1940-1942); Wilmington, Del. (1943); Frederick, Md. (1944-1945); West Palm Beach (1946-1962); Bradenton (1963-1969); Mesa (1969-1978; 2015-present); Scottsdale (1979-1983); Phoenix (1984-2014).

PEORIA STADIUM / SAN DIEGO PADRES / SEATTLE MARINERS

QUICK FACTS

- **Capacity**: 12,518 (includes 3,000 berm seats)
- **Year Opened**: 1994
- **Dimensions**: 340L, 385LC, 410C, 385RC, 340R
- **Dugout Locations**: Mariners on third-base side, Padres on first-base side
- **Practice Times**: 10 a.m. for both teams
- **Gates Open**: Two hours before game time
- **Ticket Lines**: 800/677-1227, 623/773-8720
- **Ballpark Address**: 16101 N. 83rd Av., Peoria, AZ 85382
- **Directions**: From I-10: Take Loop 101 North. Exit Bell Road (exit 14) and head east. Turn south on 83rd Avenue. Peoria Sports Complex is approximately one-quarter mile away. From I-17: Take Loop 101 West and exit on eastbound Bell Road (exit 14). From Bell Road, turn south on 83rd Avenue. Peoria Sports Complex is approximately one-quarter mile away.

PARTY TIME IN PEORIA

Don't look now, but Peoria Sports Complex is all grown up. After years of improvements and the maturation of the surrounding area, the spring home of the Seattle Mariners and San Diego Padres is among the best ballparks and training complexes in the Cactus League. With a game scheduled virtually every day, you're assured of baseball action during a visit to Peoria, a suburb of Phoenix.

In the past, we were not very big fans of Peoria Stadium. It was not an overly comfortable place to see a game, with cramped concourses, a huge threat of sunstroke, and traffic jams galore. But a two-year renovation addressed those issues, expanding the ballpark footprint while allowing Peoria to overhaul concessions. That expansion also included a new, larger team store, a new high-end restaurant, a new water feature for the young ones, and more. All in all, the improvements were well-chosen and increased capacity while at the same time dispersing traffic throughout the ballpark. Add in the general passion shown by Padres and Mariners fans for both their teams and spring training, and you have one of the more exciting atmospheres in the Cactus League.

The Peoria Stadium footprint is circular, with seating down the lines brought in and reoriented toward the infield, as opposed to the former orientation toward center field. There is a huge outfield berm seating 3,000, and it's packed most games. (Arrive early: the best spots in the outfield go quickly.) All in all, the ballpark is very accessible, has good sight lines, and can accommodate larger crowds quite nicely.

Peoria Sports Complex was the very first MLB spring-training complex totally shared by two teams. Before Peoria, there were situations where two teams played games in the same ballpark, but they maintained separate training facilities. Today, almost every new training camp in the Cactus League is built for two teams.

The first round of improvements to Peoria Stadium came in February 2014, when the city unveiled a 56,224-square-foot clubhouse for the Mariners and a 60,834-square-foot Padres clubhouse, complete with hydrotherapy rooms, dining facilities, administrative offices, indoor and outdoor batting tunnels, and shaded patios. The extensive facility allows both teams and their minor-league squads to practice simultaneously. All in all, there are 12 MLB-sized practice fields (two lighted), and four half fields.

The next round of improvements to Peoria Stadium included an expansion of the concourses and a new team store. The biggest change to Peoria Stadium in 2015 was the addition of a large, shaded group area in left field now branded as a Four Peaks bar and an adjoining group space. The bar, featuring a large selection of Four Peaks microbrews on tap, a slew of macrobrews (including plenty of tallboys), and mixed drinks, is a welcome respite for the sun-drenched fan, with drink rails, bar stools, and four tops galore. In front of the shaded bar is a group area with a great view of the field; if no group has rented it, it's open to the public.

More than any other Cactus League facility, a spring-training game at Peoria Stadium feels like a real event. There's always a lot of traffic and excitement surrounding a game—both the Padres and the Mariners draw well during spring training—and the games sport a carnival-like atmosphere. The area around the ballpark has evolved from a series of chain restaurants and generic hotels to an intriguing mix of high-end restaurants and unique eateries. The P83 Entertainment District provides plenty of options both before and after a game. (Don't worry: We'll run down its many charms later in this chapter.) The ballpark and the games are a central part of the local community: you can expect to see many members of the Peoria Diamond Club—the "Red Shirts" at games—who raise funds for local charities.

No matter who's the home team—and the first week of the season it won't matter a lot, as every spring the Padres and Mariners face off several times—you can always expect crammed seating, a berm area teeming with families and expatriates, and a busy concession concourse. The only difference may be in the fans' complexions. For some reason, San Diego residents always look tanner and healthier than their pasty Puget Sound compatriots.

If you can, definitely hit a Padres or Mariners game in Peoria: it is one of the essential experiences in Cactus League spring training.

INSIDER'S TIP
You could be navigating some serious construction in the Peoria Stadium and Peoria Sports Complex area in

2025. The city of Peoria has been pursuing a development on 17 acres of city-owned land near the Peoria Sports Complex, known as Stadium Point at P83. The plan is for a million square feet comprising a mixed-use development that includes Class A office space, residential, hotel, and parking. Work on site prep and residential units should be underway during spring training 2025, with a new hotel tentatively planned for 2026.

BALLPARK HISTORY

Peoria Stadium was built for the Seattle Mariners and San Diego Padres, first opening in 1993.

THE SPRING-TRAINING BALLPARK EXPERIENCE

CONCESSIONS

The food selection at Peoria Stadium is amazingly varied. Yes, there's the normal selection of ballpark foods—hot dogs, hamburgers, foot-long corn dogs, nachos, pizza, pop, etc. The hot dogs come in plain, foot long, and loaded versions, with interesting toppings like bacon and cheese. If your palate runs to the refined, you can seek out more exotic offerings like noodle bowls, gyros, roasted corn, BBQ, deep-fried burgers, sno cones, chicken tenders, Philly cheesesteaks, fish tacos, teriyaki chicken, and hand-dipped ice cream.

The craft-beer selection is similarly top-notch. In short, you are never too far away from a good beer selection at any point in the ballpark.

For instance: Each end of the grandstand features a micro-brew stand tied to each team (the Seattle stand, for example, is the Belltown Brewpub). Red Hook and Stone IPA are available, as well as the unique imported German grapefruit beer from Schofferhofer (yes, it's quite good). If you're not into beer, lemonade spiked with vodka is worth a search.

In the outfield concourse, you'll find the aforementioned Four Peaks Pavilion, as well as a Red Hook brewery tent. Four Peaks is probably the leading microbrewery in the Phoenix area these days (by this point you should be used to seeing references to Four Peaks). If the peach ale is on tap, jump on it.

Finally, two bomber stands offer a variety of the big bottles and tallboy cans. Take your beers over to the drink rails on both sides of the scoreboard, and you'll have a perfect view of the action. Or wander the park and find another spot; in general, the renovations added more drink rails to the mix.

INSIDER'S TIP
A new group social space is the American Furniture Warehouse Oasis, where a group can enjoy the game in a private area completed with a dedicated bartender.

If you're into a more upscale experience, consider The Colonnade at Peoria Sports Complex. During most of the year this is a 3,300-square-foot event and meeting space. During spring training, it becomes a high-end restaurant built into the grandstand with a patio seating section facing the third-base line. It's an air-conditioned space with its own restrooms and bar.

Concessions are divided up into two areas: behind the grandstand and in the outfield. Heading to the concessions behind the grandstand means you'll miss some of the action if you decide to closely peruse the offerings. The outfield concessions, while lesser in number, are pretty good, with fish tacos, Philly cheesestcaks, chicken tcndcrs, BBQ (including somc tasty pork nachos), and burgers available in several stands. If you're a homesick Mariners fan, search out the stand selling Ivar's Clam Chowder. Good food is always the order of the day in Peoria Stadium.

AUTOGRAPHS

Neither team takes batting practice in the ballpark, opting instead to warm up on practice fields closed to the public. That means players show up just before the game, entering the ballpark from the right-field corner via Autograph Alley, on the right-field concourse. Your best bet is to arrive early to the ballpark and attract a player or two to the edge of the stands or to hang out in the right-field corner and snare a player leaving the game. Players enter and leave the ballpark from this area, and many will stop and sign. Position yourself next to the wrought-iron fence and snare players as they leave the game.

The Padres tend to gather near Section 122 before a game; we've never been to a game where a few players didn't head over to sign autographs.

PARKING

Parking is $5. We used to recommend dining before a game and then walking over to avoid paying for parking, but not anymore. The P83 area is now so built up you are taking up a valuable parking spot for a bar or restaurant. So get there early (yes, the lots will fill up if there's a large crowd, and with potential construction we may see plenty more restrictions), pay for parking, and then walk to an establishment for a pre-game beer. As a bonus, there is a section of the Peoria Sports Complex parking lot reserved for RVs.

WHERE TO SIT

You have a wide array of choices for seating at Peoria Stadium, as the ballpark features a wraparound concourse and a large berm. The berm is crammed on a typical day, so arrive early and stake out a claim.

In the grandstand, you have your choice of theater-style seats (all 100-level sections, Sections 200-214, and all club-level seats in Sections 300-303) or unbacked bleachers (Sections 216-220). In general, we advise avoiding the bleachers: they're hot and uncomfortable.

INSIDER'S TIP
Section numbering starts behind home plate; odd-numbered sections are down the third-base line and even-numbered sections are down the first-base line.

INSIDER'S TIP
To sit near the Mariners dugout, shoot for Sections 105-113 (odd numbers). To sit near the Padres dugout, shoot for Section 106-114 (even numbers).

INSIDER'S TIP
There's not a lot of shade at Peoria Stadium. Your best bet for relief from the sun lies in the area around Section 208, closer to the back of the grandstand, or in the outfield enclosed area. Otherwise, you'll face lots of exposure to the sun—so bring plenty of sunscreen (no bottle; plastic tube only), hit the free sunscreen dispensers in the restrooms, or buy some in the team store.

FOR THE KIDS

This is the most kid-friendly ballpark in the Cactus League, thanks to The Cove, a play area featuring a Shipyard splash pad, pirate ship, seating for adults, and a dedicated concession stand. The space is designed to bring folks to the Peoria Sports Complex year-round (the same reason for the Colonnade), but it's a definite bonus for spring-training fans with families in tow. You can't directly see the game (easily, anyway) from The Cove, but you'll see plenty of families setting up base camp on the berm or in the Four Peaks Pavilion and sending the kids to the splash pad. On a hot day, head there for a coolness break: there are misters throughout. Also designed for the kids: two Wiffle-ball fields.

SELFIE SPOTS

Interestingly, one of the best spots for a selfie at Peoria Stadium isn't readily apparent when you first walk into the ballpark. The back of the center-field scoreboard is used as a marketing tool, proclaiming Peoria Stadium to be the home of the Padres and Mariners. It makes the perfect backdrop for a selfie.

Another great selfie spot: on the walkway to the Mariners practice fields are two large numbers, #11 and #24. The two numbers honor Edgar Martinez (#11) and Ken Griffey Jr. (#24). These are the only two retired numbers for former Mariners. (As with every other MLB team, the Mariners retired #42 to commemorate Jackie Robinson.)

IF YOU GO

WHERE TO STAY

Staying in Peoria is problematic. On the one hand, there are many hotel rooms available within two miles of the ballpark (some are located in Peoria, others in Glendale). But tour operators, who combine a hotel room with game tickets, reserve many of those rooms months in advance. The rooms that are available typically go for at least $275 or more a night —which is a lot to pay for a room during spring training. One interesting development: It appears that Peoria Sports Complex hotels are expensive and in demand throughout much of the winter and spring, so don't feel like you're necessarily being gouged because you're a spring-training fan.

To be within walking distance of the ballpark and have an affordable room, you'll need to make a hotel reservation almost a year in advance or buy a package from a tour operator. Here are five recommended places within a mile of the ballpark:

- La Quinta Inn & Suites Phoenix West Peoria, 16321 N. 83rd Av., Peoria; 623/487-1900; *wyndhamhotels.com*. This hotel is located directly next to the complex; you'll have to deal with a lot of traffic, but you'll also have a ridiculously short walk to a game. This is also the official hotel for both teams, so rooms can be scarce for much of spring training.
- Hampton Inn, 8408 W. Paradise Lane, Peoria; 623/486-9918; *hilton.com*. Again, we're talking a ridiculously short walk.

- Residence Inn Phoenix Glendale, 8435 W. Paradise Lane, Peoria; 623/979-2074; *marriott.com*.
- Holiday Inn Express, 16771 N. 84th Av., Peoria; 623/853-1313; *ihg.com*. (Be warned that this location is across the freeway from the training complex and perhaps not as walkable as you would assume.)
- Comfort Suites Peoria Sports Complex, 8473 W. Paradise Ln., Peoria; 623/334-3993; *comfortinn.com*.
- The Hotel Serene, 7885 W. Arrowhead Towne Center, Glendale; 623/412-2000; *thehotelserene.com*.
- SpringHill Suites Glendale Peoria, 7810 W. Bell Rd., Glendale; 623/878-6666; *marriott.com*.

You may also decide that staying near the ballpark is not worth the extra expense. You're in luck: there's now an abundance of hotels in the West Valley, particularly along the 101 Corridor or along Bell Road toward Sun City. We cover the hotels in the Westgate Entertainment District in our Glendale chapter. There you'll find a wide range of hotels, from a Renaissance to a Home2 Suites. Along Bell Road you'll find a series of moderately priced hotels in Sun City, with easy access both to Surprise Stadium and Peoria Stadium. We cover them in the Surprise Stadium chapter.

RV RESORTS NEAR THE BALLPARK

There is an abundance of RV resorts in the general vicinity of the complex and a short drive away from the ballpark. A few are located in adjoining Sun City, and the remaining resorts close to the ballpark are located south on Highway 60, which can be a traffic nightmare. (No, there's no resort within walking distance of the ballpark.) In general, these resorts are geared toward snowbirds and not necessarily for short-term stays, so do some homework and call ahead before assuming there will be a spot for you. As a bonus, there is a section of the Peoria Sports Complex parking lot reserved for RVs during games, but not for overnight parking.

WHAT TO DO OUTSIDE THE BALLPARK

There are some who decry the suburban nature of Peoria, and indeed the area surrounding the ballpark does have a strong suburban feel, as chain restaurants sit comfortably next to local establishments. There are many outstanding restaurants within walking distance of the park. Most are located across 83rd Avenue, a short walk from the ballpark. (Peoria is marketing this area as P83, which you may see in some promotional materials.) There's been quite a bit of turnover in the area in recent years, so your fave from five years ago may be out of business. You can walk to all of these restaurants from Peoria Sports Complex. The increase in traffic in P83 has cut down on open parking in the area, as establishments want to maintain spots for their customers. This is a very pedestrian-friendly area, so we'd recommend parking at the ballpark and then walking to your destination.

Recommended: Firebirds Wood Fired Grill. A mix of upscale food in a rustic environment, Firebirds draws big crowds, especially on the weekend, with steaks and cocktails the big draw. *Firebirds Wood Fired Grill, 16067 N. Arrowhead Fountains Center Dr., Peoria; 623/773-0500;* **firebirdsrestaurants.com**.

A great breakfast spot close to the ballpark: Hash Kitchen. Any spot with Hangover Hash and bloodies on the menu is the perfect way to start out a weekend day at the ballpark.

*Hash Kitchen, 16222 N. 83rd Av., Peoria; 623/352-4990; **hashkitchen.com**.*

You'll find a marriage of cultures at Headquarters Grill Bar Sushi: sushi meets pulled pork meets sports bar. Yes, that does translate into something for everyone. A bonus: with 50 HD TVs, you're likely to find any game you want during March Madness. *Headquarters Grill Bar Sushi, 16041 N. Arrowhead Fountains Center Dr., Peoria; 623/547-5577; **headquartersaz.com**.*

Another sports bar worth checking out: The Moon Saloon, with an abundance of beers, TVs, and March Madness devotees. We'd recommend the fish and chips. Interestingly, The Moon has been claimed as a Chicago hangout by White Sox and Cubs fans, so don't be surprised if there's a large crowd there before and after games involving a Chicago team. *The Moon Saloon, 16554 N. 83rd Av., Peoria; 623/773-2424; **themoonsaloon.com**.*

One more notable sports bar: Bubba's 33, an indoor-outdoor spot with plenty of TV screens on the walls and lots of burgers on the menu. Camp out for your March Madness fix. *Bubba's 33, 16100 N. Arrowhead Fountains Center Dr., Peoria; 623/412-9933; **bubbas33.com**.*

The Social on 83rd is another casual spot in the P83 area, with an eclectic menu featuring the likes of short rib tacos, hamburgers, and paninis. *The Social on 83rd, 8350 W. Paradise Lane, Peoria; 623/486-4343; **thesocialaz.us**.*

Revolu is one of those trendy taquerias popping up in urban areas, focusing on street food and high-end tequilas. It's patterned on Tijuana street scenes—something that should be familiar for San Diego-based spring-training visitors, albeit with a few twists: try the Mexi-meatballs as an appetizer. Definitely ask to sit on the patio. *Revolu Modern Taqueria + Bar, 15703 N. 83rd Av., Suite 110, Peoria; 623/878-0215; **revolutaqueria.com**.*

If you want something more mainstream, there are a number of chain restaurants close to the ballpark, including Red Robin, Famous Dave's, Buca di Beppo, Giordano's, P.F. Chang's, Cheesecake Factory, Texas Roadhouse, In-N-Out Burger, Chipotle, and MOD Pizza.

There are also some establishments worth visiting farther afield of P83.

Padre Murphy's is a long-established sports bar in the Valley, combining a slew of craft beers, affordable daily specials, and enough televisions to please every March Madness fan. As a bonus, Padre Murphy's throws a blow-out St. Patrick's Day event under a parking-lot tent. *Padre Murphy's, 4338 W. Bell Rd., Glendale; 602/547-9406;* **padremurphys.com***.*

You'll find some Padres fans before and after games at Oggi's. (Of course, Oggi's is headquartered in southern California, so the link isn't that absurd.) Microbrewed beers and trendy designer pizzas are featured. *Oggi's Sports | Brewhouse | Pizza, 6681 W. Beardsley Rd., Glendale; 623/566-8080;* **oggis.com***.*

Peoria has turned into the site of some pretty decent brewpubs, though none are particularly close to Peoria Stadium. Still, after a matinee game, you may find these brewpubs are worth the drive. Peoria Artisan Brewery (*10144 Lake Pleasant Pkwy., Peoria; 623/572-2816;* **peoriaartisanbrewing.com***)* is known for its IPAs and amber beers. Go for the deviled eggs. Richter Aleworks (*8279 W. Lake Pleasant Pkwy., Peoria; 602/908-6553;* **richteraleworks.com***)* offers a limited selection of beer, both brewed onsite and elsewhere.

Worth the drive: Arrowhead Grill, a high-end steakhouse known for its 10-ounce Delmonico, lovingly slathered in lemon butter, and the 48-ounce porterhouse (really). Don't let the Glendale address fool you: it's less than two miles from Peoria Stadium. Drive north on 83rd Avenue and then hang a right on Union Hills Drive. *Arrowhead Grill, 8280 W. Union Hills Dr., Glendale; 623-566-2224; **arrowheadgrill.com**.*

In addition, you're close to the Westgate Entertainment District (covered in our Camelback Ranch–Glendale chapter), which has its own set of charms.

SPRING-TRAINING HISTORY: SAN DIEGO PADRES

The San Diego Padres have trained in Arizona since their National League inception in 1969. The team trained in Yuma from 1969 to 1993, moving to the new ballpark in Peoria in 1994.

SPRING-TRAINING HISTORY: SEATTLE MARINERS

The Seattle Mariners have trained in Arizona since their American League inception in 1977: from 1977 to 1993 the team trained in Tempe, while in 1994 the team moved to the new ballpark in Peoria.

SALT RIVER FIELDS AT TALKING STICK / ARIZONA DIAMONDBACKS / COLORADO ROCKIES

QUICK FACTS

- **Capacity**: 11,000
- **Year Opened**: 2011
- **Dimensions**: 345L, 390LC, 410C, 390RC, 345R
- **Dugout Locations**: Diamondbacks on third base, Rockies on first base
- **Gates Open**: Two hours, 10 minutes before game time. Home BP, to 11:15 a.m.; visitors BP, 11:15 a.m.-12:15 p.m.
- **Ticket Lines**: 888/490-0383 or 480/362-WINS (9467)
- **Address**: 7555 N. Pima Road, Scottsdale, AZ 85258
- **Directions**: From Loop 101 (Pima Freeway) northbound: Take exit 44 (Indian Bend Road) and turn left, proceeding west for approximately 0.6 miles. Turn right at N. Pima Road. From Loop 101 (Pima Freeway) southbound: Take exit 43 (Via De Ventura) and turn right, proceeding west for approximately 0.8 miles. Turn left at N. Pima Road.

STATE OF THE ART IN SCOTTSDALE

It's the only spring-training ballpark to be built on tribal land and the most popular when it comes to attendance. It's also a great place to take in a game, representing the state of the art in spring-training facilities. Unless you're truly strapped for time or don't want to venture past a favorite facility, a visit to Salt River Fields at Talking Stick should be on the agenda for anyone visiting Phoenix for Cactus League action.

For decades, the approach to a spring-training facility was pretty static: there was a main ballpark where games were played, with a couple of open fields for practices, drills, and minor-league workouts. The widely accepted premise was, if it was good enough for Connie Mack at Fort Myers' Terry Park in 1925, it was good enough for every other MLB team.

But designers of more recent spring-training facilities have moved away from this model. The new goal for architects and team management is to integrate what fans love about spring training—player access, warmer weather, a relaxed atmosphere—with the daily functionality of the complex. The HKS Sports & Entertainment Group first addressed these issues with Camelback Ranch–Glendale, which opened in 2009, and reinvented them at Salt River Fields at Talking Stick.

That approach is apparent when fans first draw near the complex. Instead of herding fans to one or two ballpark entrances, Salt River Fields at Talking Stick gives them four different and distinct entrances. The ballpark is placed at the center of the complex, allowing fans to meander through practice fields before the game. Large angled roofs provide plenty of shade. The berm is the largest in spring training, providing space for 4,000 fans to do what they really love at spring training: grab a cold one and sprawl out in the sun. Want to just hang out? There are tons of spots on the concourse, especially beyond the bases, to just sit down and relax. With running water on the west side of the complex, the ballpark feels like an oasis, especially on a hot spring day. Add to that a strong presence from the Salt River Pima-Maricopa Indian Community (SRPMIC)—the project hosts—and you have a unique spring-training environment.

How strong? The history of the Maricopa and Pima tribes is displayed prominently at the ballpark. Restroom signage is in three languages: Maricopa and Pima tribal languages as well as English.

There are some similarities between Camelback Ranch and Salt River Fields. Both place the ballpark in the center of spring action and surround it with training facilities. And both rely on lots of natural finishes and colors. But Salt River Fields takes the lessons and extends them further with some local touches. There's plenty of shade in and around the ballpark in the form of ramadas. And there's no blocky ballpark exterior wall; fences guide your way.

More than most spring-training complexes, Salt River Fields is designed for leisurely strolls. Between the walk from the parking lot to your seat via the training fields to the 360-degree concourse, fans are not expected to sit for nine innings. Time really does stand still at a ballgame, especially at Salt River Fields. Take a walk. Take a break at the one of the many seating spots on the concourse and visit with a friend. Buy a beer or head to the margarita stand for a cold one. You'll never actually miss the game, as you can view the action from the concourse at all times.

If it sounds like we recommend a visit to Salt River Fields at Talking Stick: we do, wholeheartedly. A trip to the Cactus League wouldn't be the same without a trip to a Diamondbacks or Rockies game.

INSIDER'S TIP
There are four entrances. Many fans will enter the ballpark from a main entrance behind home plate after crossing a bridge over a water feature, while other fans will enter at the center-field gate, nearest the most parking. (The water feature is also functional: recycling water for future use on the playing fields.) There are ticket offices at all four gates, as well as Will Call windows at all four gates. You don't need to circle the ballpark to find a Will Call window if you've ordered tickets online, but you will need the correct window if a friend or ticket service has dropped off ducats for you.

INSIDER'S TIP
Diamondbacks and Rockies home games start at 1:10 p.m. or 7:10 p.m.

INSIDER'S TIP
In previous years Salt River Fields and Sloan Park jointly hosted a primo college-baseball event after players report but before games start: The MLB Desert Invitational, featuring the likes of BYU, California, Grand Canyon University, Ohio State, and USC. No word at 2025 press time as to schedules and matchups.

THE SPRING-TRAINING BALLPARK EXPERIENCE

CONCESSIONS

Most of the stands offer the ballpark basics: huge hot dogs (including seven variations at Home Plate Hot Dogs, which also serves a Beyond Meat burger), burgers, pizza, ice cream, and more. The Talking Stick Mega Dog is a half-pound foot-long topped with pork and mac and cheese, and there is the inevitable bacon-wrapped Sonoran Dog. A dedicated barbecue stand offers up pulled pork and a BBQ trio plate, as well as pork carnitas tacos. (Yes, check them out: they're an interest mix of carnitas with lime-scented cabbage and cilantro crema.) To be honest, we're of mixed opinion on the PB&J burger from the Cattle Company stand: it combines a half-pound burger with peanut butter and sweet chili jam (hence the PB&J), topped with jalapeños, cheddar cheese, and bacon. The national headquarters for Cold Stone Creamery is to the north of the ballpark on Via de Ventura (alas, it's just a standard-issue office building, not a Wonka-esque shrine to the fine art of ice-cream making), so there's the requisite Cold Stone ice cream available. And there is the inevitable Thai Island Noodles stand, which has somehow become a spring-training staple. If you need some caffeine, stroll to the center-field Dutch Bros coffee stand. We also recommend the Ike's Love and Sandwiches stand along the third-base line, a mainstay at Hohokam Stadium that's made its presence known throughout the Valley with multiple outposts.

INSIDER'S TIP

We can't guarantee any of these items will return in 2025, but in 2024 fans saw these new choices on the Salt River Fields menus: burrito bowls, smash burgers, a bacon mac and cheese dog, and Italian nachos.

INSIDER'S TIP

The 400-capacity Pepsi Patio at the top of the grandstand has one big selling point: you'll have a great view of virtually every mountain of note surrounding the Valley of the Sun, including Red Mountain and the Four Peaks. It's the best party spot in the Cactus League, featuring bar stools, drink rails, high tops, and an abundance of flat-screen TVs, perfect for monitoring during March Madness—all for $28.

Worth seeking out: margaritas served at stands run by local vendors, as well as vodka lemonades and sangria at dedicated concourse stands. (In fact, there are some folks who head to the ballgame and spend all of their time watching the action from the right-field concession stand seating.) It's hard to miss the sangria stand and the dedicated Jack Daniels and Absolut stands on the main concourse. Also worth seeking out: lobster rolls from the Cousins Maine Lobster food truck.

The beer selection is OK: mixed in with AB InBev and MillerCoors craft beers (Leinie, Blue Moon) are some legitimate craft beers. Paying $14 for a tallboy is perhaps the most distressing part of a Salt River Fields visit.

INSIDER'S TIP

No outside food is allowed in Salt River Fields at Talking Stick. You can, however, bring in two sealed water bottles.

INSIDER'S TIP

Yes, being the credit cards and ditch the Benjamins: Salt River Field is a cashless venue.

AUTOGRAPHS

Trails lead to the back practice fields from the ballpark, where you'll occasionally find some minor-leaguers working out. The practice fields have some interesting names. The Diamondbacks fields, on the Desert part of the complex, are named Devil's Claw, Jackrabbit, Mesquite, Quail, Ramada, and Whirlwind. The Rockies fields, located on the Mountain side of the complex, are dubbed Adobe, Cottonwood, Dust-storm, Red Clay, Red Mountain, and Wild Horse.

When in the ballpark, Diamondbacks and Rockies players are encouraged to sign autographs at the edge of the seating along Sections 101-104 (Rockies) and Sections 120-123 (Diamondbacks); they usually start 40 minutes before the game and stay through the National Anthem. On most days, players will sign in those same locations after the game as well. This is a tradition, it seems; we witnessed the same sort of behavior from D-Backs players when the team trained in Tucson.

Players have also been known to hang out and sign autographs for kids after the game. Don't be a Comic Book Guy with your binders and binders of cards, elbowing your way ahead of some kid seeking an autograph.

Finally, both teams held a noon autograph session on the

left-field concourse on most game days, the D-Backs in the left-field corner and the Rockies in the right-field corner.

PARKING

Parking is plentiful in the four lots adjoining the ballpark; the site can host 3,000 cars. The cost is reasonable: $5. You can park a little closer to the ballpark for $10, or go valet for $20. The complex also runs shuttles from one end of the parking lot to the ballpark if there is a huge crowd. Plenty of folks park in the neighboring shopping center and walk over to the complex's south entrance.

FOR THE KIDS

A supervised Cold Stone Creamery Kids Fun Field Wiffle-ball diamond opens an hour before the game. On Sundays, kids can run the bases after the game.

WHERE TO SIT

There are 7,000 theater-style seats at Salt River Fields, while the berm has a capacity of 4,000—the largest in spring training.

Really, there's not a bad seat in the house. Sure, the seats down the line are farther from the action, but you have the advantage of sitting close to the bullpens and autograph areas. The sun is an issue down the third-base line, of course.

The ballpark orientation is askew from the traditional north-east baseline configuration to allow for more shade during an average 1:10 p.m. game time. This puts more seats in the shade: out of the 28 rows in the grandstand (16 in back of the main aisle, 12 in front), 85 percent of them will be shaded at some point in the game. In the back, you'll find an abundance of shade; the 12 rows in the front portion of the grandstand start in the sun and will be in the shade for the end of the game. And yes, there are sunscreen dispensers at the ballpark, located at the Bud Light Seltzer Lawn.

INSIDER'S TIP
Sections are numbered in a clockwise manner: Section 101 is the first section down the first-base line, while Section 123 is the last section down the third-base line. While both sit far from the action, they each have an advantage: they sit next to the home bullpen.

INSIDER'S TIP
The Diamondbacks dugout is down the third-base line, and the Rockies dugout is down the first-base line. To sit near the D-Backs dugout, go for Sections 115-120; to sit near the Rockies dugout, go for Sections 104-109.

SELFIE SPOTS

Logos are affixed to the team buildings past the outfield concourse, which makes for a nice backdrop. In addition, the team names are affixed to the exterior entryways for both teams; they, too, make nice backdrops.

IF YOU GO

WHAT TO DO OUTSIDE THE BALLPARK

The Talking Stick Resort is across Highway 101 from the ballpark, providing Indian-style casino gambling, as well as a host of bars and restaurants. (More on it in the next section.)

The Talking Stick brand extends to the Pavilions at Talking Stick, a shopping center south of the ballpark. It's been revitalized in the last several years and now features some very good restaurants and quick-service establishments, ranging from Angry Crab Shack and Red Robin to Chipotle and Starbucks. It also features a Target for all your post-game shopping needs.

Worth a stop, especially as a chance for a learning moment with your kids: the USS Arizona Memorial Gardens at Salt River, which honors the brave individuals serving aboard the USS Arizona that sank on December 7, 1941, during the attack on Pearl Harbor. It pays tribute to and recognizes the individuals aboard the ship that day; sharing their stories, their efforts and their sacrifice. The Salt River Pima-Maricopa Indian Community became the recipient of a large part of the superstructure of the USS Arizona (BB-39), identified as the original Boat House, and built the Gardens around it in just six months. The Boat House relic was part of the original memorial built at Pearl Harbor in 1951 and is the largest and only piece ever given to a tribal community. The USS Arizona Memorial Gardens at Salt River spans the exact length and width of the USS Arizona with over 1,500 commemorative columns, representing those aboard the ship on December 7, 1941. In addition, there are gaps within the column outline representing an individual who survived the attack. As the day ends, each column illuminates, transforming the memorial at night. The project extends across the entry drive of Salt River Fields to the north and juts into the lake on the south. (The address: 7455 N. Pima Rd, Scottsdale.) The Gardens are open daily from dawn until dusk and is open and free to the public.

A popular pre- and post-game spot for both Salt River Fields and Scottsdale Stadium game-day attendees is the Vig McCormick Ranch, billed as an upscale neighborhood tavern, complete with plenty of outdoor seating and a menu strong on comfort food. *The Vig McCormick Ranch, 7345 N. Vía Paseo del Sur, Scottsdale; 480/758-5399; thevig.us.*

A relaxed, upscale spot: Grassroots Kitchen & Tap, notable for a Southern-inspired menu, Happy Hour, and patio seating. Head here right after the game and hang out for a couple or so hours. *Grassroots Kitchen & Tap, 8120 Hayden Rd., Suite E-100, Scottsdale; 480/699-0699; grassrootsaz.com.*

You are only five miles away from downtown Scottsdale, which we covered in depth earlier in this book. To get there from the ballpark, go south on Pima to Indian Bend Road and turn right. Drive a mile west to Hayden Road, then turn left and drive for 2.5 miles until you reach downtown Scottsdale.

Also adjacent to the ballpark area: a Medieval Times outpost. Part restaurant, part dinner theater, Medieval Times makes every day a Renaissance Festival day. You can expect knights jousting in a castle-themed environment, complete with falconry, equestrian demonstrations, and a royal court. If eating without utensils and watching knights joust to an imagined conclusion sounds appealing, then the national dinner chain is for you. *Medieval Times, 9051 E. Vía de Ventura, Scottsdale; 866/543-9637; medievaltimes.com.*

WHERE TO STAY

The Talking Stick Resort is across Highway 101 from the ballpark. (No, not really within walking distance.) The 496-room/suite hotel features a 240,000-square-foot casino, two championship-level golf courses designed by Ben Crenshaw and Bill Coore, two pools with private cabanas, and several restaurants. The Talking Stick Resort is part of the SRPMIC development efforts. This is by far the nicest accommodation close to the ballpark. *Talking Stick Resort, 9800 E. Indian Bend Road; Scottsdale; 480/850-7777; talkingstickresort.com.*

Speaking of the restaurants at Talking Stick: A good place to head after the game is the 15th-floor Orange Sky Lounge, which features even more spectacular views of the McDowells and Camelback Mountain. Sit on the patio and enjoy the view.

At The Pavilions at Talking Stick, across Hummingbird Lane from the Colorado Rockies entrance to the ballpark: Staybridge Suites (*9141 E. Hummingbird Ln., Scottsdale; 480/291-5175; ihg.com*). The family-oriented hotel should be sold out for much of spring training: combine large suites with a location within walking distance to the ballpark, and you can't go wrong.

Similarly close: Comfort Suites Scottsdale Talking Stick Entertainment District (*9215 E. Hummingbird Lane, Scottsdale; 480/476-7600; choicehotels.com*) is a family hotel located close to the ballpark. If you can get a get a room here within your budget, grab it.

Also appealing to families: Great Wolf Lodge, the first in the Phoenix area. Born in the Wisconsin Dells, the Great Wolf Lodge chain combines high-end family-oriented suites (some 350 in all here) with waterpark and entertainment areas. In the case of the Scottsdale Great Wolf Lodge, the 85,000-square-foot indoor waterpark features a variety of body slides, tube slides, raft rides, activity pools and splash areas. The adjacent 27,000-square-foot family entertainment center, the Great Wolf Adventure Park, features arcade games, miniature golf, and rope courses, as well as the unique Magi-Quest live-action adventure game where players use interactive magic wands to solve mysteries and track down prizes. (Yes, we've done it; yes, the kids will love it.) A lobby show with Great Wolf characters will entertain the kids before bedtime. One of the nice things about a Great Wolf Lodge: admission to the water parks is limited to those staying in the lodge, ensuring a more secure and less crowded environment. *Great Wolf Lodge, 7333 N. Pima Road, Scottsdale;* **greatwolf.com.**

Another unique offering in the Talking Stick area: Salt River Hotel at The Block, within a short drive of Salt River Fields. Located at The Block at Pima Center at Via De Ventura and the 101 freeway, Salt River Hotel features a noteworthy four-story wood frame construction housing a dual-Hilton brand hotel. One side of the building includes 85 guest rooms under the Home2 Suites brand, including a kitchenette with a midsized fridge, kitchen sink, and a microwave with counter space. The other side of the building includes 81 guest rooms under the Tru brand. Marrying these two concepts is interesting: Home2 Suites appeals to families traveling on a budget, while the Tru brand features small rooms nestled in a hipster environment. *Salt River Hotel, 8401 N. Pima Center Pkwy., Scottsdale;* **hilton.com.**

Within a short drive: the Hampton Inn & Suites Scottsdale-Riverwalk. Corporate all the way, but quiet and clean. It's also a very short drive to the Talking Stick Resort. *Hampton Inn & Suites Scottsdale-Riverwalk, 9550 E. Indian Bend Road, Scottsdale; 480/270-5393;* **hilton.com.**

Given your location, however, you could easily stay at almost any Scottsdale resort or downtown hotel and be within a close drive to the complex. In addition, the many airport hotels are under 10 miles away. There's something at every budget level, ranging from the high-end resorts like The Phoenician to midrange affordable hotels farther from downtown.

INSIDER'S TIP
Given that most Diamondbacks live in the area, the team doesn't maintain an official spring hotel. The Rockies do: The Scottsdale Plaza Resort (*7200 N. Scottsdale Rd., Scottsdale; 480/948-5000;* **scottsdaleplaza.com**).

Interestingly, you'll also find some Cubs folks there as well.

SPRING-TRAINING HISTORY: ARIZONA DIAMONDBACKS

The Arizona Diamondbacks have trained in Tucson (1993-2010) and Scottsdale, Az. (2011-present).

SPRING-TRAINING HISTORY: COLORADO ROCKIES

The Colorado Rockies have trained in Tucson (1993-2010) and Scottsdale, Az. (2011-present).

SCOTTSDALE STADIUM / SAN FRANCISCO GIANTS

QUICK FACTS

- **Capacity**: 12,000
- **Year Opened**: 1992
- **Dimensions**: 360L, 430C, 330R
- **Dugout Location**: First-base side
- **Practice Times**: Workouts begin at 9 a.m.
- **Gates Open**: Gates open two hours before game time. Giants batting practice, 10:15-11:15 a.m.; visitors batting practice, 11:15 a.m.-12:15 p.m. Add five hours for a 6:05 p.m. game.
- **Ticket Line**: 877/4SF-GTIX (877/473-4849)
- **Address**: 7408 E. Osborn Rd., Scottsdale, AZ 85251
- **Directions**: The ballpark is located at Osborn Road and North Drinkwater Boulevard (formerly Civic Center Drive), two blocks east of Scottsdale Road. There are plenty of signs pointing the way. If you lose your way, follow signs to two ballpark neighbors: the Scottsdale Civic Center and Scottsdale Healthcare.

A SOUTHWESTERN ATMOSPHERE IN SCOTTSDALE

A San Francisco Giants game is an essential spring-training experience, and downtown Scottsdale is one of the trendiest areas in the Valley. With a slew of bars, restaurants, shops, and arts offerings, a typical downtown Scottsdale experience is a day-long affair. And during spring training, that typical downtown Scottsdale experience is likely to include an afternoon or evening at the ballpark, sandwiched between a morning of shopping, an afternoon Happy Hour, and an evening dinner at a great local eatery. You should plan on devoting a full day to walking the streets of downtown Scottsdale and taking in a Giants game.

Scottsdale bills itself as being a true Wild West town, but that's merely the façade of the epicenter of upscale Phoenix. Scottsdale has a totally different look and feel than the rest of the Valley of the Sun. There's some genuine history in downtown Scottsdale, and over the years the area has evolved from being a kitschy little outpost outside of Phoenix to an affluent suburb. When you visit Scottsdale Stadium, be prepared to do some battle with BMW sedans and Audi convertibles on the roadways.

The centerpiece in the spring is Scottsdale Stadium. While the ballpark has been improved over the years, the site has hosted spring training since the opening of the original 1956 Scottsdale Stadium, the former Cactus League home of the Baltimore Orioles, Boston Red Sox, Chicago Cubs, and Oakland A's. It features 8,500 fixed seats, with room for 2,000 on outfield berms and group areas. With a pleasant Southwestern design scheme and an efficient layout, Scottsdale Stadium is one of the hottest tickets in the Cactus League.

What did fans see at Scottsdale Stadium the past few springs? A new clubhouse and event center on the Osborn Road side of the ballpark, at the east end of the parking lot and basically in the right-field corner; an expanded right-field Charro Lodge with a new upper deck; widened concourses to allow better traffic flow throughout the ballpark; new bleachers and standing-room space added to the right-field concourse; an overhauled press box; and an expanded main entry. The main entry is now an inviting spot to hang out and meet friends before a game. It's also a spot for a selfie or two, with public art by Craig Smith from the collection of the City of Scottsdale. New ticket windows at this main entry also make for a smoother entry process into the ballpark.

The changes address one of the biggest complaints about Scottsdale Stadium: the seating and atmosphere may be good, but it could be hard to make your way around the ballpark. Now, fans can view the action from many different and unique viewpoints. Most fans will want to camp out in the grandstand seating, which is fairly shaded from the Arizona sun, but for those wanting a more casual viewpoint there's a picnic area down the third-base line and more. There really is not a bad seat in the house.

INSIDER'S TIP
The outfield berm is a great place to watch a game. Be prepared for a steep walk out there, though. Our favorite spot in the outfield is in center field; you have your own craft-beer stand. And yes, you do need a ticket for specific areas within the berm. You can't buy a grandstand seat and then camp out there.

The ballpark atmosphere is relatively subdued—instead of the loud rock music blaring before a game, you'll hear an organist.

Another great thing about Scottsdale Stadium is its location: downtown Scottsdale. Your best bet is to arrive early to the game and park for free in a city-owned covered parking ramp directly north of the ballpark. Your car will enjoy the respite from the hot Arizona sun, and you'll have a chance to walk the two blocks to downtown Scottsdale, where there are a number of shopping and dining establishments. Otherwise, there's usually plenty of street parking in the general vicinity. Downtown Scottsdale is very safe, so don't be afraid to leave your car in an area marked for longer-term parking.

INSIDER'S TIP
Scottsdale Stadium is also home to the Arizona Fall League Hall of Fame and the Scottsdale Sports Hall of Fame. The Arizona Fall League is where major-league teams send prospects after the regular season to play under elite conditions, and members of the AFL Hall of Fame include the likes of Todd Helton and Derek

Jeter. The Scottsdale Sports Hall of Fame honors notable locals, including Jim Palmer.

The San Francisco Giants are a major draw for spring training. The local community supports the team, Giants fans still make the trek to Scottsdale, and the ballpark environment is one of the best in the Cactus League. When a traditional rival is in town—like the A's or the Chicago Cubs—the place is packed. Be sure to buy your tickets well in advance.

WORKOUTS

The Giants train at Scottsdale Stadium. Workouts start at 9 a.m. Most of the time the major-league squad can be found in the ballpark, while an adjacent workout field is also used. After games start and the Giants have an away game scheduled, workouts are scheduled for 10 a.m., a good time to snare autographs.

Minor league players work out within a newer complex at the Papago Sports Complex in Phoenix, at the site once used by the Oakland Athletics for their minor-league camp. If you ever attended A's spring-training workouts at the Papago Sports Complex, you remember it as a very basic, dusty facility at best. The new facility features six workout fields, including one with the outfield dimensions of Oracle Park and one with the dimensions of the team's former home, Candlestick Park. Also part of the training complex: A spiffy new building with new rehab facilities, additional bullpen mounds, new batting cages, and a new training/weight room. And, we're guessing plenty of development tech behind locked and guarded doors. All of this is the result of a $50-million investment from the Giants. The complex is at the northwest corner of North 64th Street and East McDowell

Road in Phoenix, just across from Scottsdale. The entrance is on the 64th Street side. *1802 N. 64th Street, Phoenix.*

THE SPRING-TRAINING BALLPARK EXPERIENCE

CONCESSIONS

The entire playing field is basically ringed by concession stands. Several beer and food portables are located in back of the berm. And a brat and beer stand is located in the left-field corner, affording you a view of the game and the opposing bullpen as you scarf down a grilled delight. That stand features its own high-tops and views of the action.

This tends to lead to an abundance of riches. In general, the concessions at the ballpark are pretty well laid out, and there is certainly no avoiding them. Each section has its own concessions area, so you should plan on grabbing food on the way to your seat. Larger concession stands with ballpark staples like hot dogs, brats, pizza, beer, and hamburgers are located in the back of the grandstand. Or you can take a break from the action and bring some good food down to the many picnic tables located down the left-field line. These tables do not have a view of the action, although they are located closest to specialty concessions stands. Plan your concession trips. Before the game, the concourses are very crowded as everyone grabs a beer and a dog. After the game starts, the concourses are much less crowded.

Among the more notable offerings: roasted sweet corn, garlic fries, John Morrell hot dogs (the Giant Dog is great), Johnsonville brats, Philly cheesesteaks, grilled burgers, garlic fries, barbecue, chicken tenders, and street tacos. There are the obligatory Four Peaks selections, of course.

AUTOGRAPHS

Head early to the ballpark before a day game if you're seeking an autograph, as the Giants set up a designated autograph area outside the clubhouse at two times: 9-11 a.m. and 30 minutes before the first pitch.

Within the ballpark, Giants players are pretty good about coming over to the first row of seats and signing autographs. A proven spot is Section 129, so head there when you arrive at the ballpark. Also, Giants players will stop in the walkway next to the dugout (leading to the clubhouse) near Section 118 and sign autographs before the game, while pitchers will stop and sign a few outside the home bullpen. Visiting players tend to congregate between their dugout and the bullpen.

INSIDER'S TIP
Protective netting runs down each foul line.

PARKING

Arrive early to score a free parking spot at Civic Center Parking Garage, the covered parking ramp directly north of the ballpark, next to the public library on Drinkwater Boulevard. (The main shaded level has a time limit; the upper level does not.) From there you can walk into the ballpark or a few blocks to Old Town Scottsdale. As a bonus, many of the entrepreneurs reselling tickets set up shop outside the parking ramp. The Giants are a great draw, and most games come close to selling out.

Otherwise, there are many ramps and lots close to the ballpark, including the Parking Corral at East 2nd Street and Brown Avenue, but there's more than enough free street parking in the area as well if you're prepared to walk. We've never had issues parking in downtown Scottsdale on a game day. One thing when it comes to street or ramp parking: do take note of the posted parking times. At the Civic Center Parking Garage's main floor, you're limited to three-hour parking between 10 a.m. and 5 p.m.—and the ramp is patrolled.

INSIDER'S TIP

You don't need to park near the ballpark; you can catch the free Downtown Scottsdale trolley to the ballpark. The shuttle runs from Scottsdale Fashion Mall, leaving every ten minutes and makes a loop through downtown Scottsdale and Old Town. Stops at Scottsdale Stadium are added for spring training. It runs from 90 minutes before each game until 30 minutes after the end of the game. For more information, call 480/312-3111 or visit *scottsdaleaz.gov/trolley*.

You may also consider a cab or rideshare service to get to and from Scottsdale Stadium. A dedicated lane on the ballpark's west side makes pickups and dropoffs a breeze.

WHERE TO SIT

The outfield berm is a popular spot and is usually crammed for every game. It's a mix of high-end and no-frill seating at a wide range of pricing, including the Charro Lodge, an all-inclusive seating area behind the Giants bullpen in right field. It's not cheap, costing $90 to $150 depending on the opponent, but it is a nice oasis in a very frenetic ballpark, offering all-you-can-eat deals. Recent renovations added even more shade, this time to the upper level. Berm seating frequently sells out, so ushers will be checking to make sure you have the correct ticket—no crashing the berm if you hold a seat in the grandstand.

There are three levels of seating at the ballpark. In Sections 101-130 and Sections 200-216, you'll enjoy theater-style seating. In Sections 300-316, you'll find bleachers with backs. In Section A-H, you'll find bleachers with no backs. As there are more bleachers than theater-style seats at Scottsdale Stadium —and the chairbacks are largely taken up by season-ticket holders—chances are good you'll be sitting on a bleacher.

INSIDER'S TIP
The seat numbering at Scottsdale Stadium puts Sections 101 and 102 directly behind home plate, with even-numbered sections down the first-base line—next to the Giants dugout—and odd-numbered sections down the third-base line. To sit near the Giants dugout, go for an even-numbered section between Section 106 and Section 118.

If you need or want shade, your choices are limited to 300-level sections, between Section 300 and Section 310. At the beginning of an afternoon game, only the back of those sections is in the shade.

SELFIE SPOT

The new clubhouse on the first-base side sported a "Welcome to Spring Training" graphic in 2020 and 2021. The public art at the entrance also serves as a fine background for your IG account.

IF YOU GO

WHERE TO STAY

Scottsdale is a great hotel town. In recent years many chain offerings have been upgraded to the boutique-hotel class. Add the resorts outside of downtown, and you have a great assortment of lodging options to choose from. All the major chains are represented in downtown Scottsdale, and they are all fine facilities. But there are some unique offerings to consider.

Your first call should be to the Hotel Valley Ho, an impressively retro facility that has been linked to spring training for decades. This was the spring base for the Chicago Cubs when that team trained in Scottsdale in the 1960s, and it's still a favorite base for Cubbies fans on spring break. The hotel opened in 1956 and retains a lot of that Eisenhower-era ambiance, though it's been modernized since; turquoise remains the color of choice in many rooms. Go for the retro feel, stay for the pool and spa, and have a nightcap (or breakfast) at the ZuZu Lounge. It's not exactly close to the ballpark, so plan on driving or calling an Uber for a ballpark transport. *Hotel Valley Ho, 6850 E. Main St., Scottsdale; 866-882-4484;* **hotelvalleyho.com**.

Another former Cubbie hangout in Scottsdale was the Hampton Inn, later transformed into the trendy Hotel Indigo. It's undergone another change to an Aloft, a millennial-aimed offering from the Marriott chain. It is very popular in spring training. *Aloft Scottsdale, 4415 N. Civic Center Plaza, Scottsdale; 480/253-253-3700;* **marriott.com**.

In past years, the official team hotel was the Hilton Garden Inn Scottsdale Old Town; it's still a solid choice for spring-training fans, within a pleasant short walk to the ballpark. *Hilton Garden Inn Scottsdale Old Town, 7324 E. Indian School Rd., Scottsdale; 480/481-0400;* **hilton.com.**

Five other hotels are within a half-mile of the ballpark, giving you the chance to set up camp and walk to the ballpark every day. Comfort Suites is typical of that budget chain; just be prepared to pay a premium if you can get a room. *Comfort Suites Old Town, 3275 N. Drinkwater Blvd., Scottsdale; 480/946-1111;* **choicehotels.com.**

The Courtyard by Marriott belies that chain's reputation as a mid-priced location and charges more than $300 nightly during spring training, if you can snare a room. *Courtyard by Marriott Scottsdale Old Town, 3311 N. Scottsdale Rd., Scottsdale; 480/429-7785;* **marriott.com.** Similarly corporate and similarly situated: the Holiday Inn Express and Suites. It's popular, clean, and easily accessible—what more do you need? *Holiday Inn Express, 3131 N. Scottsdale Rd., Scottsdale; 877/863-4780;* **ihg.com.**

A more upscale offering is the Saguaro Hotel, located north of the ballpark on Indian School Road. The Saguaro chain is as boutique as it gets; if you can't take a dose of attitude with your room (like a work desk adorned with a framed portrait of Roy Rogers), you probably should pass. But with every room sporting a balcony and a restaurant, El Jefe Cantina, with a patio overlooking Civic Center Mall, the Saguaro Hotel just screams retro Scottsdale. Bonus: use one of the hotel bicycles to pedal to the game. *The Saguaro, 4000 N. Drinkwater, Scottsdale; 877/808-2440;* **thesaguaro.com.**

A good choice for families is the Extended Stay America in Old Town Scottsdale, which features kitchenettes and multi-bedroom accommodations. *Extended Stay America, 3560 N. Marshall Way, Scottsdale; 480/994-0297;* **extendedstayamerica.com.**

The newest of the hotels located within a half-mile of the ballpark: the high-end Canopy by Hilton Scottsdale Old

Town in the Arts District, with a sleek decor aimed toward millennials and those wanting a luxurious pool experience. *Canopy by Hilton Scottsdale Old Town, 7142 East 1st St., Scottsdale; 480/590-3864;* **hilton.com.**

There's a large assortment of lodging in the greater Scottsdale area, so you should not feel compelled to stay in downtown Scottsdale. Resorts in Scottsdale are among the best in the world. We like two in particular:

- The Camelback Inn is a flagship resort for the Marriott chain, featuring over 450 casitas (essentially, guest houses) with private patios. Before or after the game you can sun yourself beside one of the three pools. It's not cheap—try getting a room under $500 per night—and it does sell out. *Camelback Inn, 5402 E. Lincoln Dr., Scottsdale; 800/242-2635;* **camelbackinn.com.**
- The Phoenician, another Marriott flagship property, is a pure luxury resort featuring a 27-hole championship course. You'll pay for the privilege of being away from the madding crowds, but you'll get a truly upscale experience with renovated rooms. *The Phoenician, 6000 E. Camelback Rd., Scottsdale; 800/888-8234;* **thephoenician.com.**

RV RESORTS NEAR THE BALLPARK

The price of Scottsdale real estate pretty much precludes the presence of any RV parks close to the ballpark. We'd recommend looking to Mesa for any RV park with halfway decent proximity to Scottsdale Stadium.

WHAT TO DO OUTSIDE THE BALLPARK

The ballpark is directly adjacent to the Marshall Way Arts District, which includes the Scottsdale Civic Center, the Scottsdale Center for the Arts, and the Scottsdale Museum of Contemporary Art. The mall between these buildings is a nice calm spot and well worth a stroll before the game. Right off the mall is a slew of restaurants and watering holes. You will not go hungry or thirsty while in downtown Scottsdale.

Otherwise, we cover the charms of the area in our Phoenix overview and the section on Scottsdale.

SPRING-TRAINING HISTORY: SAN FRANCISCO GIANTS

The San Francisco Giants' franchise has held spring training in the following locations: New York City (1901-1902); Savannah, Ga. (1903-1905); Memphis (1906); Los Angeles (1907, 1932-1933); Marlin, Tx. (1908-1918); Gainesville, Fla. (1919); San Antonio (1920-1923, 1929-1931); Sarasota (1924-1927); Augusta, Ga. (1928); Miami Beach (1934-1935); Pensacola, Fla. (1936); Havana (1937); Baton Rouge (1938-1939); Winter Haven (1940); Miami (1941-1942, 1946); Lakewood, N.J. (1943-1945); Phoenix (1947-1950, 1952-1980); St. Petersburg (1951); and Scottsdale (1981-present).

SLOAN PARK / CHICAGO CUBS

QUICK FACTS

- **Capacity**: 15,000 (9,200 fixed seats, 4,200 outfield-berm capacity, 1,600 suite-level seating)
- **Year Opened**: 2014
- **Dimensions**: 360L, 366LC, 410C, 398RC, 360R
- **Dugout Location**: First-base side
- **Practice Times**: Practices begin at 9 a.m.
- **Gates Open**: Grandstand opens two hours before game time. Cubs batting practice (at next-door administrative facility), 10:10-10:55 a.m.; visitors batting practice, 11 a.m.-noon.
- **Ticket Line**: 800/THE-CUBS
- **Address**: 2330 W. Rio Salado Pkwy., Mesa, AZ 85201
- **Directions**: The ballpark is southeast of the Hwy. 202 and Hwy 101 interchange on E. Rio Salado Parkway. From Phoenix and points west: Take Hwy. 202 and head east. Take exit 8 (McClintock Dr.) and go south to E. Rio Salado Parkway. From

Scottsdale and points north: Take Hwy. 101 south to
Exit 52. Turn left (east) on E. Rio Salado Pkwy.
From Tempe: Take E. Rio Salado Pkwy. east.

WRIGLEYVILLE IN THE DESERT

As a celebration of the Chicago Cubs past and present, Sloan
Park is an attractive venue for any sort of baseball fan. You
don't need to be a hardcore Cubs fan to appreciate the exterior murals showing the evolution of the Cubs branding or
the interior design touches invoking Wrigley Field. And you
don't need to be a hardcore Cubs fan to appreciate the shaded
seating or the top-notch concessions. True, many of the fans
inside Sloan Park *are* hardcore Cubs fans, and they're more
concerned about Dansby Swanson's health and the status of
the starting rotation than the total fan experience. That's OK:
you'll have a great time anyway.

Attending a Cubs spring-training game has always been a
must for all sports fans, no matter where the team played.
Indeed, the Cubs perhaps have the most interesting spring-
training history in all of baseball, and the unprecedented
success at Sloan Park is just another noteworthy occasion in
the team's long history.

The Cubs have had one of the most geographically diverse
spring-training histories of any MLB team, with bases
ranging from Avalon Park on Catalina Island (California) to
Long Beach to Mississippi to Tampa to Scottsdale and Mesa.
Former Cubs owners William Wrigley Jr. and Philip Wrigley
weren't shy about leveraging the Cubs against their other
business investments, and so over the years baseball needs
were secondary to promotional and personal needs. (We'll
discuss some of them later in this chapter.) In recent years,
team ownership has settled for basic facilities like
Rendezvous Park, Fitch Park, and Hohokam Park for training

and games. When Sloan Park opened in 2014, the team finally had a spring facility capable of generating enthusiasm from fans.

INSIDER'S TIP
The ballpark opened as Cubs Park. In January 2015 the Cubs sold naming rights and a Wrigley Field sponsorship to Sloan Valve Company, resulting in the current moniker.

Sloan Park is located in Mesa, but this isn't the same part of Mesa as Hohokam Stadium, spring home of the Athletics and the former Cubs spring home: it's part of a larger park area right on the edge of Tempe. It's not the most scenic of sites, with a water-treatment facility and a freeway serving as a grandstand backdrop. (Fans down the first-base line do have a decent view of the Superstition Mountains, however.) It's also not one of the most accessible locations, either, with just one four-lane road—Rio Salado Parkway—providing east-west access, and many streets in the area close on game day, funneling vehicles to Rio Salado Parkway. (In other words, plan ahead and be prepared to wait in line for a parking spot before the game or to leave the ballpark after the game.) Streets do encircle the ballpark—Clark on the west, Sheffield on the east—and fans will probably drive around Sloan Park to view workouts and check out the facility on a non-game day.

INSIDER'S TIP
Speaking of parking: We advise approaching the ball-park from the east, past Riverside Park. (Feel free to come early: the park has also been renovated as part of the ballpark development and features a climbing wall and towers of various heights, a splash pad, and a lake stocked with fish. This area is also home to a Sheraton hotel.) General parking is to the east of the ballpark, while reserved/handicapped parking (the so-called red parking because of the red stripes placed on reserved and media passes) is to the west and south of the ballpark. Yes, there will be lines, and yes, there will be a wait.

The Cubs' spring-training facility is in two parts, albeit in the same block. Sloan Park is separate from a 65,000-square-foot administrative facility with 10,000 square feet of workout space, multiple clubhouses, team offices, rehab facilities, meeting spots, and more. The workout space is spacious, with the latest in workout gear on two levels and plenty of Cubs branding within, including championship banners, logos on the actual workout machines, and a huge mural of Wrigley Field at one end. The workout area opens up via garage doors to a football field (yes, football fields are big in training facilities) and a shaded space. Multiple practice fields are to the west and east of the building. If you're going to watch a practice, this is where you'll go: the main training field is open to the public on one side, with some limited seating on hand.

The team dresses in this administrative space and then walks to the ballpark via a dedicated roped-off area before the game. It's not too daunting a barrier, and spring-training fans have plenty of opportunities to snare a player or 10 for an autograph before the game. Expect a crowd waiting to see the Cubs enter the ballpark.

INSIDER'S TIP

You can enter the ballpark from any gate no matter your seat location, and there are three on the south side of the ballpark. Before the game, take a minute to walk along the south side of Sloan Park (the side facing Rio Salado Parkway) and check out the montage of Cubs logos and other retro Cubs touches on the ballpark exterior. The Cubs have always been the best-branded team in baseball, and a look at the changes in the Cubs logos over the years is a nice reminder of that history.

Once in the ballpark, fans will be treated to lots of shade, plenty of (but not too many) Wrigley Field touches, and high-end concessions and amenities.

The Wrigley touches are there, but not overwhelming. The same type of bricks used in Wrigley Field have been installed in the backdrop as well as on the suite level. The lighting supports on the grandstand mimic those used at Wrigley Field, and there's plenty of steel on the second level to remind folks of the Friendly Confines. A clock atop the videoboard is the same design as the center-field scoreboard clock at Wrigley. The outfield dimensions are exactly the same as

Wrigley Field. The pitch of the berm resembles the pitch of the fabled Wrigley Field bleachers.

The biggest fan attraction with a direct tie to Wrigley Field: a replica of the famous marquee installed at ground level down the right-field line. Fans can request a custom message on the marquee and take a picture with their names displayed to the crowd. Yes, there will be lines of fans wanting to send a marquee photo home—but it's well worth the wait.

One more tie to Wrigley Field: bleachers in the outfield. The berm, which seats some 4,000, was designed with the same incline as the famous Wrigley Field bleachers, to emulate the Friendly Confines feel. Past that is a left-field structure, with concessions and restrooms on the ground level and seating on the top. It's quite a distance between the action and the Budweiser Rooftop seats, but the Cubs enhanced the rooftop experience with four sections of seating—two sets of bleachers, two sets of covered four tops—and plenty of concession stands. You need a special Budweiser Rooftop ticket to be up in this area, but once you're there you'll find plenty of room at the four tops. (Warning: it's a sun field out there, and it gets pretty toasty on the bleachers. Be sure to use some of the free sunscreen, located in dispensers near the restrooms.) The whole point is to mimic the Wrigley Field rooftop experience.

INSIDER'S TIP
If you want to be near the bullpens, head for the berms. Both are located on field level beyond the home-run fence, with the Cubs in left field and the visitors in right field.

Finally, we have the seating bowl and grandstand. The second level features suites and two 400-capacity event spaces at each end. Most fans will be assigned to one of the 9,000 seats within the 15,000-capacity ballpark, but expect the concourses to be crowded: lots of drink rails ensure plenty of fans will be hanging out in the back of the grandstand, watching the game with shade and a cool breeze coming in from behind home plate. (The grandstand was obviously designed to allow in as much breeze as possible. It does.) Those drink rails are where SRO ticket buyers congregate as well, allowing the Cubs to draw beyond ballpark capacity. The Cubs and architect Populous designed the ballpark to feature plenty of shade in the grandstand: they estimate 60 percent of the seating is shaded at the beginning of the game, thanks to canopies over every section of grandstand, including two freestanding seating areas with their own canopies down the first-base line, with that number increasing to 70 percent by 2 p.m. For the 1:05 p.m. game time, that estimate would appear to be correct: by 12:30 p.m., all seats between the dugouts are in the shade, save the first four rows behind the home dugout. Sections 103-104 were partially in the sun as well. You'll also be in the shade at the concession areas behind home plate.

But you do pay a price if you sit in the most shaded seats: the last four rows down the third-base line have serious limitations. Overhang means you won't see the outfield scoreboard, though basic displays in the bowl shows scores, balls, and strikes. Even though this is spring training, fans do keep score and want to hear the substitutions and other game information.

The fans have spoken, making Sloan Park the top draw in the Cactus League. With lots of shade, top-notch concessions, and a very Cubs-centric atmosphere, a day trip to Sloan Park is mandatory for anyone visiting the Valley of the Sun for spring-training action. The one thing from Wrigley that couldn't be replicated in the new ballpark? No ivy on the outfield wall.

INSIDER'S TIP

Plan an early trip to Sloan Park. The Cubs and the Dodgers will launch the 2025 MLB season on March 18-19 in Tokyo. That means an earlier opening when the players report and a truncated game schedule, with the last Cactus League game set for March 11.

THE SPRING-TRAINING BALLPARK EXPERIENCE

CONCESSIONS

The food at Sloan Park have mandatory Chicago roots, including the obligatory Chicago Dog, the inevitable Sonoran Dog, or the almighty Old Style tallboy. We can remember the days when Chicago wasn't a Bud town, but rather an Old Style town, and the fact the Cubs still serve Old Style—in a tallboy, no less!—is a nice acknowledgement of that past. Also worth a search at the Dos Gringos bar in the right-field concourse: Goose Island 312. If Old Style or Goose Island isn't to your taste, there are plenty of domestic macrobrews (Budweiser, Michelob) and some mega imports (Corona, Dos Equis) at the World of Brews stand in left field. Again: you're never too far from a beer stand.

These delicacies aren't found at every concession stand, so you may need to take a walk between innings to find them. The main concession stands are located behind the seating bowl, but the concourse features plenty of portable stands as well. (Tip: great food and shorter lines can be found in the left-field burger bar and center-field concessions.)

There is food at the ballpark beyond the concessions

stands as well. A dedicated citrus grove past right field features space for the popular food trucks, some shade, and picnic tables: it's fenced off so you don't need to leave the park to grab a bite. A kids' play area is adjacent, and because both areas are just beyond the concourse, parents can see the action while letting the kids play Wiffle ball. A popular open square bar along with neighboring four tops closes out the right-field offerings.

INSIDER'S TIP
Worth a visit to the food-truck area: the Iowa breaded pork tenderloins or tacos if available.

INSIDER'S TIP
Live large with a foot-long Vienna hot dog served Chicago style, available at a portable stand on the right-field concourse. Yes, it's a lot of everything— pickle, celery salt, etc.—but so good. The vendor will split it in two if you want to share. It's next to a Dos Gringos bar, serving mixed drinks and margaritas. It can fill up long before the game starts, as the combination of shade and tequila is an irresistible draw on a hot spring day.

AUTOGRAPHS

There is no full Cubs clubhouse in the ballpark; instead, the team dresses in the adjoining administrative facility and walks over on a sidewalk connecting to the ballpark. Their entrance to the ballpark is an administrative/media entrance to the left of the home-plate gate. That sidewalk is roped off, but fans are encouraged to gather there before the game to snare autographs before the game.

INSIDER'S TIP
There are six practice fields surrounding the administrative building, but one is used for both batting practice and main team practices: the field to the east of the
building, and the one closest to fan parking and access.
The Cubs take batting practice on this field, which
features limited seating in the form of bleachers and a
small berm on the first-base side. In general, the major
leaguers practice at this field and a second adjacent
field.

The minor leaguers train at a cloverleaf of four fields—
fields 3-6—to the west of the administrative building.
There are bleachers at all four fields.

In general, Cubs players will head to the ballpark between
noon and 12:30 p.m. on the designated walkway, sometimes
riding in golf carts. Do not head into the ballpark when the
gates open at 11 a.m. and expect to head back outside to snare
an autograph: the official policy is that you're not allowed
back into the ballpark if you leave. Now, we also found that
policy isn't uniformly enforced, and we've seen ushers stamp
the hands for those seeking to dash out for an autograph. In
general, if autographs are what you seek, we recommend that
you do not enter the ballpark until you've had a chance to
work the line.

Otherwise, head to the dugouts and bullpens before a
game and attempt to flag down a player. There's nothing official at all about this approach, and it's largely hit and miss,
subject to the whims of players at any given time.

PARKING

There is plenty of parking at Sloan Park beginning at $10 (depending on the day and depending where you park). In general, the parking areas to the south are reserved for those holding handicapped passes, season-ticket holders, and VIPs —the so-called red parking because of the red stripes placed on reserved and media passes. Most of you will end up parking in the unpaved area to the east of the ballpark.

There are four gates at Sloan Park: home plate, first base, right field, and center field. If you park in the east fields, the closest entrance will be right field. However, as we noted earlier in this chapter, take the time to walk around the south side of the ballpark and enjoy the mural of Cubs logos.

And many of you will need to head to the south side of the ballpark, as the ticket office is next to the right-field gate, where you'll pick up Will Call tickets. If you don't have tickets, you can buy them at booths at the right-field and center-field gates, or the automatic ticket kiosks at the right-field gate.

WHERE TO SIT

Most fans will have theater-style seats with cupholders. The ballpark design allows for 70 percent of the seating to be shaded for most of the game.

Because of the extensive shade, you can be pretty flexible about where you sit. The Cubs dugout is on the first-base side, so anything in sections 100-110 will give you a good view of the home team.

INSIDER'S TIP

The "away" seating down the right-field line are bleachers. Nice home-field advantage for Cubs fans.

Standing room, complete with plenty of drink rails in the concourse, now basically extends all the way around the concourse. Those SRO tickets allow the Cubs to oversell ballpark seating capacity.

Like most new ballparks, Sloan Park is designed to be a neighborhood of seating areas. The sections behind the Cubs dugout is one neighborhood. The fans standing behind the stands next to first base is another neighborhood. The fans bellying up to the drink rails in the concourse is another neighborhood. The fans in the berm and the Budweiser Rooftop section are in two other neighborhoods. There are many ways to view the onfield action in the ballpark, so you'll never tire of Sloan Park.

INSIDER'S TIP
You will find some online fans complaining about the steep pitch of the berm. However, there are many dimensions directly tied to Wrigley Field at Sloan Park, and the pitch of the outfield berm is exactly the same pitch as found in the Wrigley Field outfield bleachers when Sloan Park opened.

SELFIE SPOT

Is there any doubt? In front of the Wrigley Field marquee, of course. You can even request a personalized message and use as it as a backdrop for a selfie. Also worth a look: the montage of Cubs logos on the exterior of Sloan Park.

IF YOU GO

WHAT TO DO OUTSIDE THE BALLPARK

When you finally get a chance to leave Sloan Park in the post-game snarl, you'll have two choices for your next destination; To the east (left), past Riverside Park: Mesa Riverview and downtown Mesa. To the west (right): Tempe.

Many folks will park at Mesa Riverview and then walk over to the ballpark. While we don't condone the practice, we understand it, and we hope that if you tie up a parking spot for several hours you'll have the courtesy to spend some money at Mesa Riverview before or after the game. Most of the eateries at Mesa Riverview are of the chain variety—Chick-fil-A, Chili's, Famous Dave's, Cracker Barrel, IHOP, McDonald's—but there are a few exceptions.

We'd recommend the Henhouse Care for a pregame breakfast; you can't go wrong with a hearty skillet, chicken fried chicken, or a chorizo omelette. *Henhouse Cafe, 805 N. Dobson Rd., Mesa; 480/550-7474;* **henhouse-cafe.com**. Papago Brewing, which began life with a small Scottsdale tasting room and bar, is back in the form of a Mesa outpost under Huss Brewing ownership, with 60 or so craft beers on tap. The new Papago is housed in the former Brass Tap; it's good to see a local home for the delightful Orange Blossom Ale. *Papago Brewing, 1033 N. Dobson Rd., Suite 104, Mesa; 480/219-9922;* **papagobrew.com**.

We cover downtown Mesa in our Athletics chapter; check it out. Visit **downtownmesa.com** for more information.

In general, Main Street east of Hwy. 87 is where you'll find the better restaurants in the city: a mix of Mexican eateries, coffee shops, and Diamond's Sports Grille (*161 N. Centennial Way, Mesa; 480/844-3888;* **diamondssportsgrille.com**), a decent sports bar formerly known as Harry and Steve's Chicago Grill. Harry, of course, was Harry Caray, and Steve was his broadcast partner, Steve Stone. Hence the Chicago in the Desert atmosphere. The Cubs player murals are still on the wall, but there are few Chicago-themed foods on the menu.

Another Mesa sports fan hangout doesn't have any curb appeal—it's part of a relatively anonymous strip mall—but with 30 tap beers and portraits of local sports heroes, the Woodshed II (or, as known by the locals, The Shed) runs Happy Hour specials until 7 p.m., perfect to fill that time between the end of the game and dinnertime. *The Woodshed II, 430 N. Dobson Rd., #13, Mesa; 480/844-7433;* **woodshedaz.com.**

Heading west of the ballpark is your best bet for a wide selection of food and drink, as you're a short drive from the many offerings of downtown Tempe and environs. We cover those offerings in more depth in our Los Angeles Angels chapter. We do have special recommendations west of the ballpark, like Tempe Marketplace. Many of you will pass it on the way to the game, as it's located on West Rio Salado Parkway and pretty impossible to miss. There are a slew of restaurants there for any level of fan or family, but Chicago fans will want to check out two Chicago mainstays with Tempe outposts: Portillo's and Lou Malnati's. True, not like home—but close enough.

The Thirsty Lion is a sports-bar chain with an eclectic menu, featuring everything from scotch eggs to brick-oven pizza to fish tacos. An extensive beer list and craft cocktails makes it worth a stop. *Thirsty Lion Gastropub and Grill, 2000 E. Rio Salado Pkwy., #104, Tempe; 480/968-2920;* **thirstyliongastropub.com.**

It's a little off the beaten path in an area filled with low-slung industrial buildings, but Spinato's serves some of the best pizza in the Valley. The combination of sweet tomato sauce and an outstanding tavern-style thin crust will please even the most hardcore deep-dish fan cheering on his or her Cubbies. (Here's a secret: Most Chicago natives prefer the square-cut tavern pizza of their youth, not a deep-dish pie.) *Spinato's Pizzeria, 96 S. Rockford Dr., Tempe; 480/967-0020;* ***spinatospizzeria.com.***

Finally: Four Peaks Brewing Co., a brewpub and restaurant known for its patio, fresh beer (quaff a Hefeweizen if it's on tap), and good food. Expect a crowd, even if you're visiting during spring break. *Four Peaks Brewing Co., 1340 E. 8th St., Tempe; 480/303-9967;* ***fourpeaks.com.***

INSIDER'S TIP

Cubs fans follow their team on the road; for many Valley teams, some of their biggest crowds of the year occur when the Cubs come to town. When the Cubs take on the Mariners or the Padres in the West Valley Peoria Stadium, a popular Cubs fan gathering spot before or after games in the The Moon Saloon, with an abundance of beers, TVs, and March Madness devotees. It's part of the P83 entertainment district and within walking distance of the ballpark. *16554 N 83rd Av., Peoria; 623/773-2424;* ***themoonsaloon.com.***

WHERE TO STAY

Two hotels are part of Wrigleyville West, a development between Sloan Park and Riverview Park: The Sheraton Mesa Hotel (*860 N. Riverview, Mesa; 480/664-1221;* ***marriott.com***) and the Courtyard by Marriott Mesa (*2224 W. Rio Salado Pkwy, Mesa; 480/590-8000;* ***marriott.com***). Different price points and different levels of luxury here. The Sheraton Mesa was listed as a team hotel in 2024, as was Homewood Suites by Hilton (*66 S. Rockford Dr., Tempe; 480/966-2780;* ***hilton.com***).

You can either choose to stay close to the complex in what

appear to be some marginal hotels or just pick out a nice hotel in Tempe or farther abroad in Mesa and make it your base. There are several hotels within two miles of the complex (which, depending on your tolerance for the sun, may or may not make them walkable), such as a Rodeway Inn or a nicer Hyatt Place. Extending your area to three or four miles—which would put much of Tempe in your search—opens the door to a much wider selection of nicer and affordable hotels. Recommended: the Hyatt Place Phoenix/Mesa (*1422 Bass Pro Dr., Mesa; 480/969-8200; hyatt.com*), less than two miles from Sloan Park. As a plus, you'll be close to a Bass Pro Shops and the Mesa Riverview retail development, complete with lots of big-box retailers, a movie theater, and a variety of restaurants. *Mesa Riverview, 1061 N. Dobson Rd., Mesa; mesariverview.com*.

RV RESORTS NEAR THE BALLPARK

The ballpark is in the northwestern part of Mesa, putting it a decent distance from the many RV parks in eastern Mesa and Apache Junction.

And there is an abundance of them, to be sure. Mesa is known in some circles as being the RV park center of the Phoenix area. That's not necessarily a bad thing. There are at least 16 RV parks in the greater Mesa area, and that's not counting those in Tempe, Gilbert, Chandler, and Apache Junction. Check out the likes of Mesa Regal, Sun Life, TowerPoint or the four other Mesa resorts under the Cal-Am Resorts umbrella (*cal-am.com*), or the camps offered by Encore RV Resorts (*rvonthego.com*), but be warned that in general the RV resorts in Mesa are really geared more toward monthly snowbirds than weekly campers.

SPRING-TRAINING HISTORY: CHICAGO CUBS

The Chicago Cubs have trained in a variety of locations: Selma, Alabama (1900); Champaign, Illinois (1901-02, 1906); Los Angeles (1903-04, 1948-1949), Santa Monica (1905); New Orleans (1907, 1911-1912); Vicksburg, Miss. (1908); Hot Springs, Ark. (1909-1910); Tampa (1913-1916); Pasadena, Cal. (1917-1921); Catalina Island, Cal. (1922-1942, 1946-1947, 1950-1951); French Lick, Ind. (1943-1945); Mesa (1952-1965, 1979-present); Long Beach, Cal. (1966); Scottsdale (1967-1978).

Why Avalon on Catalina Island? Catalina Island is located 20 miles off the California coast, near Los Angeles, and Cubs owner William Wrigley Jr. bought a majority interest in the island in 1919. Wrigley then constructed a ballpark on the island to house the Cubs in spring training: This was the original Wrigley Field. (The ballpark is long gone, but a clubhouse built by Wrigley to house the Cubs exists as the Catalina Country Club.) By 1951 the team had grown disenchanted with Catalina Island, however, and spring training was shifted by Philip Wrigley to Mesa after the Cubs held a profitable series of games against the New York Yankees in Arizona. At the time Mesa was not seen as an attractive area for spring training, and in fact the Oakland Oaks of the Pacific Coast League failed to draw at all when the team held spring training at Mesa in 1952.

INSIDER'S TIP

Interestingly, William Wrigley Jr. also owned the Arizona Biltmore, which we discussed in our Phoenix and Scottsdale overview, but he never attempted to link the Cubs with a Phoenix or Scottsdale training camp. Perhaps he felt pro baseball was not a good fit with the upscale hotel, or perhaps he felt committed to Catalina Island.

The move to Mesa was promoted by Dwight Patterson, a Mesa rancher and builder who worked to bring spring-training games to the area. The Cubs were hesitant to move to Mesa with the New York Giants training only 20 miles away in Phoenix, so Patterson and a group of local businessmen formed the HoHoKams, who put up a $22,000 guarantee if the Cubs moved to Mesa's Rendezvous Park. Today the Mesa HoHoKams exist as a charity and still work as volunteers for games at Sloan Park (they're the ones wearing the straw hats and burgundy shirts, working the gates and the stands). The Athletics play spring-training games at Hohokam Stadium, and the field at Hohokam Stadium is named after Patterson. Rendezvous Park seated 3,000 when the Cubs moved there in 1952 but was expanded soon afterwards.

After the Cubs moved spring training to southern California in 1966, Mesa did not host any spring training until 1969, when the Oakland Athletics moved their training from Scottsdale. Charlie O. Finley was dissatisfied with the training facilities in Scottsdale; hence the move to Rendezvous Park. The A's were not a big draw in Mesa, however, and in 1976 Rendezvous Park was torn down.

SURPRISE STADIUM / KANSAS CITY ROYALS / TEXAS RANGERS

QUICK FACTS

- **Capacity**: 10,714
- **Year Opened**: 2003
- **Dimensions**: 350L, 379LC, 400C, 379RC, 350R
- **Dugout Locations**: Royals on third-base side, Rangers on first-base side
- **Practice Times**: Both teams hit the fields at 9:30 a.m.
- **Gates Open**: 10 a.m. opening on game days for both teams. Visitor batting practice starts at 11 a.m. no matter what team is home. Both teams take batting practice on adjacent practice fields.
- **Ticket Line**: 800/745-3000
- **Address**: 15860 N. Bullard Av., Surprise, AZ 85374
- **Directions**: Surprise Stadium is located 1.5 miles west of the intersection of Bell Road and Grand Avenue (U.S. Route 60, Exit 11). Bullard Avenue is located off of Bell Road, 1.5 miles west of Grand Avenue, or 2.5 miles east of Loop 303.

SURPRISE, SURPRISE

Nowhere is the growth of the West Valley more evident than at Surprise Stadium, spring-training home of the Kansas City Royals and Texas Rangers. When the ballpark opened over a decade ago, it was in the middle of nowhere. Suburban Phoenix had barely sprawled out that far northwest, and there was precious little within walking distance of what many considered to be one of the finer facilities in spring training.

Today, 20-plus springs after the arrival of the Texas Rangers and Kansas City Royals from the Grapefruit League, there's plenty in the general vicinity of what is a great place to see a spring ballgame: the sightlines are gorgeous, the concourses are wide, and the ballpark design is striking.

When you build in the middle of nowhere, you have a big advantage: land is cheap and there is space to sprawl. As a result, you have in Surprise Stadium a ballpark where it's easy to get around. The training complex is part of the 124-acre Surprise Recreation Complex. As noted, the concourses are wide and the ballpark footprint is certainly generous. Most fans won't see it, but the player spaces are similarly expansive. Built expressly for the Rangers and the Royals, Surprise Stadium features two 37,000-square-foot clubhouses with team kitchens, weight and training facilities, hydrotherapy rooms, and administrative offices. In addition, each team has covered batting cages, a practice infield, a football field (which is all the rage in spring training, interestingly), and six full practice fields.

Since opening in 2003, the Surprise Stadium complex has aged pretty well. Though there are complexes coming closer to the ideal spring-training situation (i.e., Salt River Fields), Surprise Stadium still works as a player-development center and as a place to catch a game. You will want to spend some time planning your visit, as both teams have turned into pretty decent draws for spring training. That wasn't the case right after Surprise Stadium opened. But it will be worth your efforts, as Surprise Stadium is one of the most pleasant venues in the Cactus League.

With the full Phoenix sun out for most games, you'll want to carefully choose where you sit. The ballpark features a main seating bowl, a second level with both seating and luxury boxes, outfield berm seating, and a concourse ringing the ballpark. The best seats in the house are on the second level of the grandstand and within the middle seven or so sections of the main seating bowl: these are the seats that are shaded for the majority of the game. The main level of seats extends all the way down each line. If the middle sections are sold out, you're better off sitting down the line as opposed to a section facing the outfield, as the seats farthest down the line are angled to give you a direct view of the ballpark.

Unlike most spring-training venues, there are cupholders at each seat, so you don't need to worry about some clumsy rowmate knocking over your $14 PBR.

The design is modern and clean. It does have a little touch of the retro that's proven to be popular in major-league parks like Oriole Park at Camden Yards, but not so much as to distract you from your spring-training experience.

Technically, you're attending a game at Billy Parker Field at Surprise Stadium. Billy Parker was a former major-leaguer who worked with youth baseball programs before his death in 2003. He played parts of three seasons with the California Angels and hit a game-winning homer in his first game. Alas, he never got to see a game in the ballpark he worked toward as a city activist.

INSIDER'S TIP
Volunteers are very important at Surprise Stadium. You can tell the 700 or so volunteers—the Surprise Sundancers—because they are wearing yellow shirts. They act as ushers and ticket takers. Be nice to them. They are there because of love of baseball and community, not because they feel the need to deal with drunken slobs trying to crash the shaded second level.

THE SPRING-TRAINING BALLPARK EXPERIENCE

CONCESSIONS

There are concession stands along the third-base concourse, with one big food court down the left-field line featuring Southwestern foods, burgers, ice cream, popular breaded pork tenderloin sandwiches, BBQ, and more. The hot dogs are worth seeking out: they may be roller-grilled, but they're plump and flavorful. They also come in a variety of variations. For instance, the High Heat Dog is topped with sriracha ketchup, jalapeno relish, pepper mustard, while the Tamale Dog is served inside a green chili tamale. The Cactus Corn Dog is a complex mix of beer batter, smoked sausage, and jalapeño honey mustard. And the Hometown Dog stand features a Kansas City dog topped with BBQ and slaw, a Texas chili dog topped with queso, a California dog topped with cucumbers topped with tzatziki, and a Arizona dog topped with pico de gallo.

Also worth checking out: a mac 'n cheese and bratwurst bowl, a bacon mac 'n cheese hot dog, a hamburger- and bacon-wrapped hot dog, toasted turkey, and more. Many food items are sold in combos, like the BBQ sandwich combo that includes fries, soda, and peanuts. In addition, there's a separate concession area in back of center field for those watching the game from the berm. It's a handy spot to load up if you're entering the center-field gate. Worth seeking out in past springs: Saigon Kitchen, the ballpark outpost of a popular Surprise restaurant. Go for the garlic noodles.

INSIDER'S TIP

We were always fans of the Legends Deck, located behind the right-field berm. In 2024 the deck was moved to the right-field concourse, without much of a view of the game but still featuring other amenities. You'll first need to buy a ticket to the game (we recommend a berm ticket) and then spend $45 more for the upgrade, but then you'll have access to food (including entrée and dessert) catered by a local restaurant, as well as a drink (beer, water, or soda) ticket.

The beer selection is much improved over recent years. It doesn't take much work to find craft beers from the likes of

Texas-based Spoetzl Brewery (Shiner Bock), Huss Brewing, Four Peaks, Goose Island, Surprise's own State 48, and Kansas City-based Boulevard Brewing on tap to go along with macrobrews like Bud and Michelob. If you want a little more kick in your cup, there's a cocktail stand down each line featuring Tito's Vodka, as well as margaritas sold in commemorative Mason jars. Bonus: all the seats have cupholders. And there are picnic tables down each line as well.

AUTOGRAPHS

The biggest flaw in Surprise Stadium is its lack of good autograph opportunities, as neither team takes the field until just before game time. Both take batting practice on adjacent and off-limits practice fields, although at times you'll see some Rangers taking batting practice on the enclosed cages across the concourse from the first-base area. Your best bet is to hit the ballpark well after the gates open and try to lure a player to the stands after they enter the field and are heading to the dugouts. Be warned that both teams enter the field from the outfield corners; they do not enter through the grandstand or dugouts. (Fans of visiting teams should note: visiting teams enter from an entrance between sections 101 and 102 and will occasionally stop to sign.) Other than that, the pickings are pretty slim before and during the game. After the game you'll occasionally see players hanging around as they walk from their dugouts to clubhouses.

PARKING

Free! 'Nuff said. There's plenty of parking next to the ball-park, and it's all free, free, free. If you arrive close to the start of the game and the main parking areas are full, you may be diverted to parking at the next-door aquatics area. You're still close to the ballpark, and the price is still right: free. If you have a ticket, head right to the marked third-base gate; if you do not, head to the ticket office near center field and enter via that gate.

Worth noting: the Sundancers often run golf carts throughout the parking area to help those who may need a little help getting to their seats.

INSIDER'S TIP

When you enter the ballpark, take a minute to reflect when you cross Buck O'Neil Way, which runs between Surprise Stadium and the parking lot. Buck O'Neil was one of the true pioneers of baseball, a crucial bridge between the Negro Leagues and MLB integration. O'Neil began his playing career in 1938 with the Kansas City Monarchs, later serving as a player-coach. After integration, O'Neil became the first black MLB coach, working for the Chicago Cubs. He later scouted for the Royals and was a fixture at Kauffman Stadium. If you saw Ken Burns' landmark *Baseball* PBS documentary, you saw the sparkling wit that made O'Neil such a beloved figure in the game.

CONNECTIVITY

Free WiFi! Once again, 'nuff said.

WHERE TO SIT

We recommend either sticking as close to the middle of the grandstand as you can afford or head to the berm. When you get down both lines—say, in Section 115 and beyond—you'll find your seats are oriented toward center field, making for an uncomfortable twist of the neck if you want to closely follow the infield action.

INSIDER'S TIP
The grandstand seating begins with Section 100 and is divided by odd-numbered sections up the third-base line and even-numbered sections up the first-base line. To sit near the Royals dugout, go for odd-numbered sections between 105 and 113; to sit near the Rangers dugout, go for even-numbered sections between 106 and 114.

There's one more reason to seek a seat as close to home plate as possible: comfort. There's an abundance of shade at Surprise Stadium: every Upper Dugout seat—Sections 201-206—is located under a roof in the upper portion of the ballpark. In addition, these sections provide the overhang that shades the rear rows in Sections 101-112. These seats are a premium, as every retiree in the area knows enough to buy season tickets there. If you can't snare an upper-level seat, you'll find more shade in the first-base section at the beginning of an afternoon game.

The berm is also a perfectly acceptable place to watch the game. It's big—seating 3,600 or so—and has its own concession stand. Bullpens are cut out of the berm down each line, so you can watch players in action as they prep for a game appearance. Plus, as there's a wraparound concourse surrounding the playing field, you can wander the ballpark to your heart's content.

That wraparound concourse makes it easy for those physically challenged to make their way to handicapped-accessible seating in the back of sections 101, 102, 107-112, and 117-120. In addition, there is handicapped seating behind each bullpen in the outfield.

SELFIE SPOT

As with most Cactus League ballparks, there are some outstandingly scenic vistas outside the ballpark. To see the White Tank Mountains from the ballpark—or to capture them in the background for a nice selfie—position yourself in the right-field berm.

IF YOU GO

WHAT TO DO OUTSIDE THE BALLPARK

Surprise is on the far edge of the Phoenix metropolitan area, and the growth in the area over the past several years has been impressive, to say the least. On the one hand, you're out in suburbia: the area is currently a mix of housing develop-

1

ments (the original Sun City development is due east, while new Sun City developments are within the city limits to the west), big-box retailers, and plenty of strip malls. When Surprise Stadium opened, it was in the middle of nowhere. And while you can still see nowhere from the ballpark (just look past Sun City Grand to the west), there's a lot more of note within a short drive of the ballpark than there was a decade ago.

As noted earlier, State 48 Brewery beers have been sold at the ballpark, but you can also head to their stylish brewpub before or after the game. We'd recommend Happy Hour or dinner after a matinee, especially at a patio table. With over 20 beers on tap, a covered patio, and an extensive menu featuring plenty of dishes prepared from scratch, State 48 Brewery is worth a post-game visit. *State 48 Brewery, 13823 W. Bell Rd., Surprise; 623/584-1095;* **state48brewery.com**.

Several years ago, chains dominated the restaurants close to the ballpark, but these days you can find something a little more unique and regional within a very close drive. Places we can recommend include Saigon Kitchen (*14071 W. Bell Rd., Surprise; 623/544-6400;* **saigonkitchenaz.com**), Rito's (*15643 N. Reems Rd., Surprise; 623/546-3835;* **ritosmexicanfood.com**), and Babbo Italian Eatery (*15609 W. Bell Rd., Surprise; 623/825-1919;* **babboitalian.com**). They have served Saigon Kitchen dishes at the ballpark, but you'll find favorites like lemongrass chicken and garlic noodles here as well. In addition, there are several more chain restaurants at the corner of Bell Road and Highway 60 east of the park.

Sure to be rocking on St. Patrick's Day: The Irish Wolfhound Restaurant & Pub (*16811 N. Litchfield Rd., Surprise; 623/214-1004;* **irishwolfhoundpub.com**). No, we can't explain the inexplicable popularity of Irish bars in the Valley of the Sun, past the fact that many retirees like to include a beer and some camaraderie in their daily routines, but the Irish Wolfhound usually attracts a crowd after a game.

Worth a little farther drive is Macayo's Mexican Kitchen. The Macayo's Mexican Kitchen chain dates back to 1948 and goes past a standard menu of tacos and burritos with specialties like chicken poblano and grilled salmon. *Macayo's Mexican Kitchen, 6012 W. Bell Rd., Glendale; 602/298-8080;* **macayo.com.**

Surprise Stadium exudes a strong family vibe, so a predictable popular post-game destination is Uptown Alley, which features a 40-lane bowling alley, 80 games, a laser-tag arena, and plenty of food and beverage options, including multiple bars. *Uptown Alley, 13525 N. Litchfield Rd., Surprise; 623/975-PLAY (7529);* **uptownalleysurprise.com.**

In addition, you're a reasonable drive from Peoria or even Glendale. We'd recommend checking out the Peoria Stadium and Camelback Ranch–Glendale chapters for more bar, restaurant, and hotel recommendations.

WHERE TO STAY

As the area around the ballpark has grown, so have the hotel choices in the area. There are three hotels within walking distance (under a mile) of Surprise Stadium:

- Residence Inn Phoenix NW/Surprise (*16418 N. Bullard Av., Surprise; 866/599-6674;* **marriott.com**)
- Holiday Inn Express Surprise (*16540 N. Bullard Av, Surprise; 855/799-6861;* **ihg.com**)
- Hilton Garden Inn Surprise (*16601 N. Stadium Way, Surprise; 855/618-4697;* **hilton.com**)

All three hotels will run you $250 or more a night during spring training, and apart from the ballpark there's not a lot within walking distance of the hotels, save the municipal complex with an aquatic center and library. In the past the Rangers put up some players and staffs at these hotels, impacting room availability, but it appears the opening of a player dorm within their area of the training complex lessened demand.

INSIDER'S TIP
The Royals team hotel in 2024 was the Wigwam Golf Resort & Spa (*300 E. Wigwam Blvd., Litchfield Park, 623/935-3811; **wigwamarizona.com***), a 400-acre, 331-room complex with three 18-hole championship courses.

Because there are so many spring-training venues in Phoenix and you're more than likely visiting more than one venue, chances are pretty good that you don't necessarily need to be staying close to the ballpark, unless all you want to do is order takeout pizza evenings after the games. Phoenix is a relatively easy area to make your way around, so don't feel like it's essential you stay close to the park. There are an abundance of cheaper chain hotels in Surprise as well as nearby Peoria and Glendale.

SPRING-TRAINING HISTORY: TEXAS RANGERS

The Texas Rangers have trained in a variety of locales: Pompano Beach, Fl. (1961-1985), Port Charlotte, Fl. (1986-2002), Surprise (2003-present).

When the "new" Washington Senators entered the American League in 1961, they established a spring-training camp in Pompano Beach, Florida, and stayed there until 1986, when operations were shifted to Port Charlotte, Florida. (That Pompano Beach ballpark lasted for several years before being torn down in 2008.) The Rangers moved spring training from Florida to Surprise in 2003. Meanwhile, the Port Charlotte ballpark was renovated and is now the spring-training home of the Tampa Bay Rays, Charlotte Sports Park.

SPRING-TRAINING HISTORY: KANSAS CITY ROYALS

The Kansas City Royals have trained in a variety of locales: Fort Myers, Fl. (1969-1987), Davenport, Fl. (1988-2002), Surprise (2003-present).

When the Kansas City Royals moved spring-training facilities to Arizona in 2003, it was the first time the team had not trained in Florida in team history. From 1969 through 1987, the team trained in Terry Park in Fort Myers, moving in 1988 to the brand-new Baseball City Stadium in central Florida.

Baseball City Stadium was the centerpiece of Boardwalk and Baseball, a 135-acre combination amusement park and baseball facility in Haines City. When the development opened, the 7,000-seat ballpark and the six-field training complex were considered state of the art.

The amusement park, alas, was not. Owned and managed by book publisher Harcourt Brace Jovanovich, the former Circus World didn't have the attractions to lure families from Orlando or Tampa. When HBJ restructured debt in 1987, it also closed down Boardwalk and Baseball. Eventually the amusement park was torn down and replaced with a residential development. The ballpark and ballfields sunk into disrepair after the loss of the Royals and were finally, mercifully, torn down to make way for commercial development.

Ironically, Terry Park remains popular with high-school and college teams in the spring. Baseball City Stadium, declared state of the art when it opened, is now long gone.

TEMPE DIABLO STADIUM / LOS ANGELES ANGELS

QUICK FACTS

- **Capacity**: 9,708
- **Year Opened**: 1969; renovated several times since
- **Dimensions**: 340L, 400LC, 420C, 400RC, 360R
- **Dugout Location**: First-base side
- **Practice Times**: Practice usually starts at 9:30 a.m.
- **Gates Open**: 90 minutes before gametime. Angels batting practice, 10:30-11:30 a.m. (on adjacent field); visitors batting practice, 11:30 a.m.-noon; Angels infield, noon-12:15 p.m.; visitors infield, 12:15-12:30 p.m.
- **Address**: 2200 W. Alameda Dr., Tempe, AZ 85282
- **Directions**: Take Broadway Street exit off I-10 (coming from either direction); travel west on Broadway to 48th Street; turn left; Tempe Diablo Stadium is 1/2 mile on the left. Enter ballpark parking area by turning left on Alameda.

DEVILS AND ANGELS IN TEMPE

The Cactus League is known for ballparks set in scenic locales, as the many buttes and mountains ringing the Valley of the Sun provide wonderful backdrops to game action. Tempe Diablo Stadium, spring home of the Los Angeles Angels, one of the most scenic ballparks in the Cactus League. With the Twin Buttes beyond the left-field fence, a striking Spanish-style exterior, and a relatively remote office-park location that paradoxically offers easy freeway access, Tempe Diablo Stadium is a gem, a must-visit for anyone hitting Phoenix in February and March.

The ballpark itself is very intimate, to say the least. The oldest ballpark in the Cactus League, Tempe Diablo Stadium opened in 1969 as spring-training home of the Seattle Pilots. But it's had many upgrades since, most recently in 2006, with an expanded training facility, the addition of training fields to the mix (six full fields in total), a new minor-league clubhouse, as well as a revamped entrance to the ballpark. Previously the Angels had practiced at an offsite facility. Throw in easy accessibility to practice fields, located on the other side of the parking lot from the ballpark, and you have a convenient spring-training experience.

INSIDER'S TIP
The long-awaited improvements to Tempe Diablo Stadium and the Angels training facilities will be implemented in two phases, beginning in 2025. The first round of improvements cover upgrades to the old minor-league clubhouse, which will be expanded to include a new major-league clubhouse, agility field, and performance center—the kind of expanded facility you see in almost every other spring-training camp.

Costs for these upgrades are covered by the City of Tempe and the Angels.

The second phase of the improvements will include upgrades to the fan experience. The tentative plan includes an overhauled grandstand, expanded berm and wraparound concourse, new videoboard, and the installation of more shading. Voters will be asked to approve bonding for these upgrades this November, with work set to be completed in time for the 2026 spring-training season.

The two best things about the ballpark are its location and its layout. It's easy to get to—get on I-10 south, take the Broadway Street exit, and follow the signs—and there's plenty of cheap adjacent parking. Tempe is within 10 minutes of the Phoenix airport, which makes it easy to hop into the car and hit a game right after arrival or before a late-afternoon flight. Phoenix is an easy drive from Los Angeles, which allows passionate Angels fans the chance to see their team in action at a great, intimate facility. These days the Halos are one of the hottest spring-training tickets in the Cactus League, second only to the Cubs in attendance. Plan ahead; the days of walking up and snaring a good ticket 30 minutes before game time are gone.

The layout of Tempe Diablo Stadium is certainly cramped, with most of the seating in the grandstand, roughly half armchair seats and half bleachers. There is also lawn seating in left and center field. The best seats are the box seats down the first-base line: you're definitely in a sun field, but the view of the buttes beyond the ballpark is spectacular. There's a minimum of foul territory, so you're never too far from the action—which includes rubbing elbows with pitchers warming up in both bullpens down each line.

INSIDER'S TIP
Most new ballparks feature a below-grade playing field; it's cheaper to dig down than build up. However, because the ballpark is built on the side of a hill, the main entrance to Tempe Diablo Stadium is at the top of a set of stairs. There are handicapped-accessible ramps on both sides of the entryway.

But there's a lot of life at Tempe Diablo Stadium: Angels fans fill the place up, families abound, and the focus is on the game.

THE SPRING-TRAINING BALLPARK EXPERIENCE

CONCESSIONS

Food and drink were overhauled at Tempe Diablo Stadium in 2014, when Legends Hospitality—the concessions company co-owned by the New York Yankees and Dallas Cowboys— took over operations. As a result, some of the more unique offerings at Tempe Diablo Stadium went by the wayside, replaced by standard ballpark fare. Yes, it's all filling, and it's priced similarly to concessions at other ballparks. But to our subjective eye, it's not nearly as good as in past years, when the smell of mesquite grilling dominated the proceedings.

Concessions are concentrated at the ends of concourses, where you'll find the proceedings dominated by ballpark staples—hot dogs, corn dogs, foot longs, cheeseburgers, chicken tenders, fries—and interesting offerings like wraps, rice and noodle bowls, barbeque, and wood-fired pizza. (Alas, no more Sonoran Dogs.) Most of the beer stands feature corporate beers, like Budweiser. Near Section 13 there's a stand with a wider variety of beers. There is picnic-table seating along the concourse in left field and within the "food court" area down the first-base line, and they're popular spots for those not wanting to eat a sloppy hot dog at their seats.

The Angels follow MLB rules when it comes to what you can bring into the ballpark. A liter of water is $6 a bottle in the ballpark. Bring your own sealed water and save a few bucks, or buy a few from one of the many vendors hawking water and peanuts outside the ballpark.

AUTOGRAPHS

There are six full and one half practice fields to the west of the ballpark, as well as the new clubhouse. All are accessible to fans at the beginning of spring training, with the four main cloverleaf fields featuring covered seating. The two fields closest to the ballpark, Fields 1 and 2, are reserved for the major leaguers. Practices usually begin around 9:30 a.m.

When games start, get to the ballpark early enough to hang out in the parking lot. In the past, before the game, the Angels take batting practice at the field directly next to the ballpark, then cut across the parking lot while heading to the clubhouse. Batting practice is technically closed off to fans, but you can line up along the left-field line and view the action from there. The Angels cordon off a walkway for players, but you can wait alongside it and snare some autographs. Players usually walk from batting practice to the ballpark beginning at 11:15 a.m.

Inside the ballpark, plant yourself next to sections 21 and 22. These sections are located next to the tunnel leading to the clubhouse, so players and coaches have no choice but to walk past fans here. Also, players are known to hang around the visitors' bullpen before games, so you should head down there and snag an autograph: it is located down the left-field line in foul territory. (The home bullpen is located beyond the right-field fence, to the south of the scoreboard: it's fenced off and not accessible to fans.) If you're seeking the autograph of a visiting player, head down the right-field line after the game and catch the attention of players heading for the team bus. The parking lot to the east of the ballpark is secured, so you can't seek autographs next to the bus or the right-field gate.

INSIDER'S TIP
The confines at Tempe Diablo Stadium are pretty tight,

and during batting practice—for the away team, as the Angels take BP at an adjacent field—there are many balls flying out of the ballpark. Most of what is hit past the home-run fence in left field heads into the berm, but occasionally a ball will leave the ballpark and end up on Westcourt Way, the street running behind the ballpark and up to the Phoenix Marriott Tempe at The Buttes. If you're a true ball hawk, head past the right-field home-run fence in the parking lot and wait for homers there.

PARKING

There are two main parking lots on the east and west sides of the ballpark, but in general the west lot is reserved for players, the front office, and VIPs. You'll be shuttled down to the east lot or other lots off Alameda Drive. Some businesses also sell parking, but don't be gouged. Generally, the parking offered by the Angels is cheaper ($10) than at surrounding lots. There is also limited street parking in the area, but be warned: the area is crawling with cops, and you will be towed if you're parked illegally during the day. Read the signs closely.

INSIDER'S TIP
We've had success with free street parking by arriving early and entering the ballpark area from the south, off West Southern Avenue and heading north on South 52nd Street.

You'll be directed to the front gate of the ballpark, in front of the steps behind home plate. Windows 1-6 are devoted to general sales; 7-8 are reserved for Will Call.

WHERE TO SIT

Not every seat is created equal, as there are slightly more backed bleachers than chairback seats at Tempe Diablo Stadium, with the chairbacks, complete with cupholders, installed between the dugouts. Ducats to an Angels game aren't impossible to buy, but good seats are at a premium.

You'll want to sit in the last four rows of the grandstand (rows W and higher) behind home plate or on the first-base side if you prefer to avoid the sun; a canopy covers concessions, not seats. (Try the back of section 12 for a good, shaded seat.) There are 24 seating sections at Tempe Diablo Stadium, with Section 1 beginning down the left-field line and ending with Section 24 down the right-field line. To be close to the home dugout and potential eye contact with Mike Trout, go for seats in sections 15-18. Speaking of avoidance: don't sit in sections 23 or 24, as they're angled toward center field, and your views of the infield will be blocked by fans in adjoining sections. These sections are sold cheaply as Grandstand seating (a misnomer, as these seats aren't technically part of the grandstand), but you're better off grabbing a four-top down the left-field line or camping out on the berm. Better choices are sections 21 and 22—which feature raised bleachers —while sections 1-4 and 18-20 feature bleacher seating as well.

Of course, if you want to avoid the sun altogether, you can spring for a suite on the press-box level. There are two suites at the ballpark.

One underrated area of seating: the $15 berm, which runs down the left-field line and wraps around the foul pole into left field, seating 2,300 or so. As a bonus, the berm seating overlooks the away bullpen, and there's generally a lot of room out there. And you can claim a picnic area on the concourse as well, where you get a limited view of the action.

With the ballpark featuring a raised concourse, handi-capped seating can be found at the back of sections 2-7, 9, 13, and 15-22. The Tempe Diablos have a reputation for being helpful and will run a golf cart out to transport folks who face mobility challenges.

FOR THE KIDS

Though we often observe many families at the ballpark—and let's face it, the backed bleachers are great for families, no matter what some may say—there is not a lot at the ballpark geared specifically for kids. The steep berm may pose some challenges for toddlers.

SELFIE SPOT

The best spot for a selfie is probably from your seat, with the buttes as a background.

IF YOU GO

WHAT TO DO OUTSIDE THE BALLPARK

There's really nothing within walking distance of the ballpark before or after the game, save a really good option: Top of the Rock at the Marriott Phoenix Resort Tempe at The Buttes (later we'll discuss the resort in our hotel section). With a large deck providing some great views of the Valley, Top of the Rock also sports a solid menu of farm-to-table offerings. *Top of the Rock, Phoenix Marriott Resort Tempe at The Buttes, 2000 W. Westcourt Way, Tempe; 602/225-9000; **marriott.com**.*

After Top of the Rock, there's not much else close to the ballpark. There are some fast-food joints on Broadway

(Whataburger, etc.) and 48th Street, but they're not places where you'll spend a lot of time. So you'll need to go a little afield—but not too far, really—for some great eats.

On Broadway: the old Boulders on Broadway is now branded as the SaltFire Brewing Co., an Utah-based micro brewery. It's still a beer and pizza joint, where craft beer rules. The signature pie is a Chuck Norris, compete with andouille sausage, pepperoni, bacon, meatballs, Italian sausage, and Canadian bacon. *SaltFire Brewing Co., 530 W. Broadway Rd., Tempe; 480/921-9431; **saltfirebrewingtaphouse.com***.

Keep on the sports theme with Casey Moore's Oyster House, especially on a nice day where you can take advantage of the outdoor seating adjacent to the Arizona State campus. Despite the name, this is really a sports bar, and the offerings are pub grub of a higher order—Oysters Rockefeller, cheesesteaks, etc. *Casey Moore's Oyster House, 850 S. Ash Av., Tempe; 480/968-9935; **caseymoores.com***.

If near-authentic Mexican food isn't your thing, you're in luck: downtown Tempe is a short drive away. Tempe is a college town, and as you might expect from a school with a (deserved) party reputation, there are a fair number of establishments in the downtown area for those who imbibe, mostly centered around Mill Avenue. (The university is located northeast of the training complex; to get there, head east on Broadway Road and then north on Mill Avenue.) At night you can easily wander in and out of the many watering holes and fast-food joints—and they are plentiful, good, and cheap in the Mill Avenue area.

While you can find fine dining in the Arizona State area, here are the places a spring-training fan will find most appropriate at the end of a long day in the sun.

Beer fans will want to check out Four Peaks Brewing Co., a brewpub and restaurant known for its patio, fresh beer (have the Hefeweizen if it's on tap), and good food. Four Peaks features indoor and outdoor seating areas; if you've been out in the sun for a Cubs or Angels spring-training game, don't be a hero—sit inside to avoid further sun exposure. Expect a crowd, even if you're visiting during spring break. (Parking can be a challenge, as your only option is street parking.) While you can get Four Peaks beer at the ballpark and at the airport, there is a better selection of cheaper quaffs at the original brewpub. *Four Peaks Brewing Co., 1340 E. 8th St., Tempe; 480/303-9967;* **fourpeaks.com**.

There are also plenty of brewpubs and sports bars in downtown Tempe and along Mill Avenue. Pedal Haus Brewery (*730 S. Mill Av., Suite 102, Tempe; 480/314-2337;* **pedalhausbrewery.com**) has a huge outdoor seating area and some killer beers on tap. Some great food and a good beer selection can be found in the Culinary Dropout location at The Yard at Farmer Arts District (*149 S. Farmer, Tempe; 480/240-1601;* **culinarydropout.com**).

Another oddity: pasties in Arizona. Pasties are normally associated with Eastern European immigrants—typical fare in northern Minnesota, Wisconsin, and Michigan's Upper Peninsula—but the Cornish Pasty Company takes the humble pasty and charges it up with a variety of creative fillings, including lamb vindaloo and *carne adovada*. Wash it down with a Hoegaarden White Ale or Mickey's Malt Liquor; both are on the eclectic drink menu. *Cornish Pasty Co., 960 W. University Dr., Tempe; 480/894-6261;* **cornishpastyco.com**.

If you're a history fan, head to The Chuckbox, a hole-in-the-wall at Arizona State where the burgers are cooked over an open mesquite charbroil fire and the amenities are basic, to say the least. Cash only! *The Chuckbox, 202 E. University Dr., Tempe; 480/968-4712;* **thechuckbox.com**.

We cover more Tempe attractions in our Chicago Cubs chapter. Though Sloan Park is technically in Mesa, it's near the boundary between Mesa and Tempe, and in many ways offers the best of Tempe while staying with the Cubs' Mesa roots.

WHERE TO STAY

Marriott Phoenix Resort Tempe at The Buttes is the closest hotel to Tempe Diablo Stadium, within easy walking distance of the complex. (In fact, it's not uncommon to see folks hanging out on the road up to The Buttes to catch a little game action, but the distance is a little daunting.) It's also one of the more scenic hotels in the Valley of the Sun: from the freeway it looks like some sort of futuristic neo-Wrightian extension of the butte. The extension is the Top of the Rock restaurant, and it offers some great views of the area at sunset. *Phoenix Marriott Resort Tempe at The Buttes, 2000 W. Westcourt Way, Tempe; 602/225-9000; marriott.com.*

Also within walking distance (albeit a long walk on some unfriendly terrain) is a Homewood Suites. It's billed as an airport hotel, but that claim is a stretch. *4750 E. Cotton Center Blvd, Phoenix; 602/470-2100; hilton.com.* Still under a mile from the training complex: Home2 Suites by Hilton, Phoenix Airport South (*4725 E. Broadway Rd, Phoenix; 602/414-0099; hilton.com*).

As the training complex is close to Sky Harbor International Airport, any of the airport hotels (and there are many) would be convenient, as would any Phoenix hotel, for that matter.

RV PARKS

There are no RV parks in Tempe city limits. There are plenty in Mesa; check out our Chicago Cubs and A's chapters for information.

FLYING IN

As mentioned, Phoenix Sky Harbor International Airport is close to the training facility. We discuss it in our chapter on Phoenix.

You may also want to consider flying into Tucson and then driving to Phoenix if the fare to Tucson is significantly cheaper. The drive is 117 miles and takes a couple of hours on I-10, but it has pretty views if you like desert scenery, and getting to the ballpark is convenient because of its location on the south side of the greater Phoenix area.

SPRING-TRAINING HISTORY: LOS ANGELES ANGELS

The Los Angeles Angels have trained in a variety of locales: Palm Springs, Cal. (1961-1965, 1980-1983), Holtville, Cal. (1966-1979), Mesa (1984-1992), Tempe (1993-present).

The major-league Los Angeles Angels began play in the 1961 season under the ownership of Gene Autry. (The playing field at Tempe Diablo Stadium is named for the old singing cowboy.) The team's first spring-training home was Palm Springs, where they played at the Polo Grounds, later renamed Angels Stadium. Angels Stadium still exists, hosting high-school and summer-collegiate baseball.

In 1966, the Angels partially shifted spring training to Holtville, California, and spent 10 days to two weeks at the four-diamond complex from 1966 through 1979 (splitting time with Palm Springs), before returning on a full-time basis to Palm Springs in 1980. The Angels then reverted back to a split schedule in 1982 and 1983, dividing spring headquarters between Casa Grande, Arizona, and Palm Springs. Between 1984 and 1992, the team trained in Mesa.

In 1993, Angels spring training shifted full-time to Tempe Diablo Stadium. But spring training has been played at this ballpark since 1969: On March 7, a crowd of 1,032 showed up to see the expansion Seattle Pilots defeat the Cleveland Indians, 19-7. Mike Marshall, who would later nab an NL Cy Young Award in 1974 as a reliever with the Los Angeles Dodgers, was the winning pitcher.

INSIDER'S TIP

When spring training first came to Tempe in 1969, the local Chamber of Commerce stepped in to organize everything the Seattle Pilots needed with the formation of the Tempe Diablos, a special events committee. The Tempe Diablos still play an important role in spring training, with over 100 volunteers providing game-day services as ushers, parking-lot attendants, and ticket takers. You'll know them by the straw hats with the distinctive red band. Say hi; volunteer groups like the Tempe Diablos are a vital part of what makes spring training such a unique experience.

Tempe Diablo Stadium was also the site of one of the more surreal periods in MLB history: the final days of the Pilots. Baseball was not exactly a hit in Seattle in 1969 at a former minor-league ballpark with limited capabilities, and during the offseason the owners, led by Pacific Coast League legend Dewey Soriano, tried selling the team before taking refuge in bankruptcy court. With investors led by Allan "Bud" Selig Jr. ready to buy the team, much of the discussion during spring training centered on whether the Pilots would end up back in Seattle or playing at County Stadium as the Milwaukee Brewers. (In fact, AP ran stories showing players in uniforms for both teams.) Finally, late in spring training—March 31, to be exact—a bankruptcy referee signed off on the sale of the Brewers to the Selig group, ending the short history of the Seattle Pilots. (We

discuss the situation in more depth in our Milwaukee
Brewers chapter.)

The Brewers returned to Tempe Diablo Stadium for spring
training again in 1971 and 1972 before shifting operations to
Sun City for 1973. Tempe Diablo Stadium would remain
empty in springtime until 1977, when the expansion Seattle
Mariners set up shop there. The Mariners trained there until
spring training 1993, when Gene Autry's California Angels
permanently moved to Tempe.

CHASE FIELD

QUICK FACTS

- **Capacity**: 48,633
- **Year Opened**: 1998
- **Dimensions**: 330L, 376LC, 407C, 376RC, 335R
- **Surface**: Shaw "B1K" synthetic turf
- **Local Airport**: Phoenix
- **Website**: *dbacks.com*
- **Address**: 401 E. Jefferson St., Phoenix
- **Directions**: Chase Field is located in downtown Phoenix, north of I-17 (Maricopa Highway). There is an abundance of signage directing you to the ballpark from all directions.

AN MLB PREVIEW AT THE END OF SPRING TRAINING

One big advantage to attending the end of spring training: the Arizona Diamondbacks traditionally schedule two exhibition games at Chase Field after Cactus League play and before the regular season.

For the Diamondbacks, the last Monday and Tuesday of spring training have been used to run Chase Field through its paces, while also giving players a chance to play a few home games before the real season opener. If you've not been to Chase Field, we'd recommend a visit, even if you're not a Diamondbacks fan. The D-Backs traditionally schedule the first of two exhibition games as a night game, giving you a chance to put together your own day-night doubleheader to end your spring-training adventure.

If you spend any time at all in spring training and travel from the west side of the Valley to the east side (and vice versa), you'll likely drive right by Chase Field. Similarly, if you fly in, chances are good your approach to Sky Harbor puts you right next to Chase Field. Located just north of I-17 (Maricopa Highway), the downtown ballpark is a multi-story marvel and visible for miles. Opening in 1998, Chase Field is an example of an MLB ballpark requiring a huge footprint to support a large retractable roof. (See also American Family Field, Minute Maid Park, Rogers Centre, and LoanDepot Park.) The aesthetics of the ballpark experience may suffer a little, especially on the second level, but in general Chase Field works.

Yes, the Phoenix weather in late March is usually lovely—not too hot, with low levels of humidity. But during the peak of the MLB season in July and August Phoenix is hot, with daytime temps regularly reaching the 100-degree mark. A climate-controlled ballpark is a necessity under the scorching Arizona sun.

And, as far as Chase Field providing a comfortable experience, the home of the Diamondbacks is a success. It's a cool 72 degrees no matter the conditions outside. With outfield windows that open when there are cooler conditions outside, it's not quite the closed experience you find in domed ballparks like the Trop.

True, Chase Field is showing its age. Issues with the roof prevents the team from opening it when fans are present. The seating could certainly use an overhaul, and far too much of the seating is on the upper deck, with the steep pitch a huge drawback. There's a shortage of social spaces for fans like us who love wandering around the ballpark during a game. But there's plenty to like about Chase Field if you are from out of town and not normally a Diamondbacks fan. Definitely worth a visit.

IF YOU GO

In general tickets are cheaper for the two exhibition games at Chase Field than for a regular-season match. The Diamond-backs are not a huge draw at the end of training camp, so you'll have your choice of locations and ticket prices. The better concession are on the main level, so we'd recommend checking out the sections between the dugouts if you want to splurge or the outfield bleachers if you don't. Not every concession stand will be open during these preseason exhibi-tions, but if you're on the main level you'll be close to the better offerings. Food at a Diamondbacks game is generally better than average for a ballpark, even the offerings on the $2 menu.

GETTING TO THE BALLPARK

Driving to the ballpark is easy. As we noted, Chase Field is directly north of I-17 (Maricopa Highway), and there's plenty of signage to the ballpark from any direction. In general, there's an abundance of parking next to the ballpark, either in street lots or parking ramps. For an exhibition game it will be easy to find nearby parking for $10 or under.

Depending on where you are staying, you may also want to explore ridesharing or light rail as your means of trans-portation. The Metro light-rail line runs directly next to the ballpark. If you're staying adjacent to a Metro line, it's far easier to hop on the train and head to the game. The trail runs from northwest Phoenix and downtown Phoenix through Tempe to east Mesa. In general, Valley Metro lines run every 20 minutes. We'd recommend verifying the details on the Metro website at *ValleyMetro.org*.

COLLEGE BALLPARKS IN THE AREA

PHOENIX MUNICIPAL STADIUM

It is one of the most beautiful venues in college baseball despite being one of the oldest, a ballpark tucked into the foothills of the Papago Park recreation area. What was once a dumpy, old ballpark with uncomfortable bleacher seating and a minimalist approach to comfort is now one of our favorite places to catch a baseball game, especially at night.

It seems like just yesterday that Arizona State University said goodbye to Packard Stadium and moved the Sun Devils baseball program back to Phoenix Municipal Stadium. But the move came several years ago in 2015. In the case of the Muni, the longtime home to baseball in Phoenix was available after the Oakland Athletics moved to Hohokam Stadium for 2015.

While there were some good business reasons for the Oakland Athletics to move to Hohokam Stadium, they did leave behind a venue with plenty of potential and charm. A 2004 renovation gave a sense of place to what was once an anonymous facility. There's a strong architectural tradition in Arizona going back to the days of adobe buildings, a style with an emphasis on natural building materials and integration with the buttes that dominate the area. In the case of Phoenix Municipal Stadium, accents made from decorative stones adorn the entryways of the stands, while the general feeling in the concourse echoes the Papago Park surroundings.

The Sun Devils put a lot of effort into making Phoenix Muni their own. Displays celebrate ASU baseball history, including coaches like Bobbly Winkles and venues like Packard Stadium. Gone is the old scoreboard, replaced by a videoboard. Outfield boards detail championships won by the Sun Devils, with a huge board inside listing former players. Small renovations in the past few years upgraded lighting and video displays. And with 10 sections of seats down each line covered with tarps, Phoenix Muni now feels like a much more intimate venue.

INSIDER'S TIP

Added to Phoenix Municipal Stadium in recent years: a two-story building down the right-field line containing indoor batting and pitching cages on the ground level and a wraparound deck on the second level, offering a group space, four tops, a dedicated concessions stand, and a great view of the field. If not used by a group, it's open to all.

But the best things about Phoenix Municipal Stadium are still present and enhanced. ASU plays much of its schedule with 6:30 p.m. games, and that's a perfect time to be at the ballpark. Night games at Phoenix Municipal Stadium are a special treat, as the colors on the Papago Peaks formations beyond center and left field are spectacular. There's always something special about an Arizona sunset, and the red hues of the rock formations in the Papago Park recreation area contrast nicely with the yellows and pinks of the night sky. True, the rock formations make a nice backdrop to the action during a day game as well, but at night the colors really come out.

Phoenix Municipal Stadium dates back to 1965, built to house spring training, college, and minor-league baseball. As noted, the 2015 move to Phoenix Muni was a return for ASU Sun Devils baseball, as the team played at Phoenix Muni in its early days. (Reggie Jackson hit the first homer for ASU at Phoenix Muni—out of the ballpark, no less.) In those days, this was the edge of the city, with an amusement park next door and little else.

Today, it's a much nicer experience. All of the seating is located between the foul poles (no outfield grass berm seating here), and it's a mix of chairbacks and backed bleachers. The concessions are located in back of the grandstand and down the left-field line.

ASU baseball at Phoenix Muni is a hit, with the team consistently averaging more than 3,000 fans per game. With the many night games on the Sun Devils schedule, it's easy to put together your own day-night doubleheader, with an MLB game in the afternoon and an ASU game at night. Highly recommended.

BALLPARK HISTORY

Phoenix Municipal Stadium was the home of the Triple-A Phoenix Firebirds until 1992, when the team moved to Scottsdale Stadium and played there before the arrival of the Arizona Diamondbacks. It also served as the spring home of the Los Angeles Dodgers for two weeks in 2008, when the Dodgers left Vero Beach early to play a series in Japan and then spent the remainder of spring training in Phoenix.

There's also a deeper history here. Light poles once installed at New York City's Polo Grounds are still in use at Phoenix Municipal Stadium, though several were eliminated when the park's lighting was updated to LEDs.

THE BALLPARK EXPERIENCE

CONCESSIONS

Phoenix Municipal Stadium concessions are more limited than they were in the A's days, but there's still a good selection of hot dogs, hamburgers, and other ballpark fare. Concession stands are located down each line and virtually impossible to miss. In all there are 12 concession windows, two patios, suites, and party decks.

And one thing still available at Phoenix Muni: beer. (This is an off-campus venue with a private concessionaire, after all. No pesky appearances to keep up with at an on-campus venue.) You'll encounter the main beer stand when you enter the park, with offerings that include MillerCoors products like Lite and Blue Moon. The beers are mostly on the craft level, albeit a little expensive.

PARKING

In theory there's a $5 charge for parking in a lot across the ballpark; there is no street parking, and no inclination by the local businesses to open their lots to baseball fans. Unless you're at the ballpark early, you'll be parking quite a distance from the ballpark as well, so bring your walking shoes. (We've visited the Muni when parking either was not enforced or the attendants left after the start of the game.)

SELFIE SPOT

When the ballpark was renovated for Sun Devils baseball, a whole slew of ASU-specific displays were added both inside and outside the ballpark. Those will be the best spots for a selfie or three.

QUICK FACTS

- **Capacity**: 8,000
- **Year Opened**: 1965
- **Dimensions**: 345L, 410C, 345R
- **Home Dugout Location**: First-base side
- **Ticket Line**: 480/727-0000
- **Website:** *thesundevils.com*
- **Address**: 5999 E. Van Buren St., Phoenix, AZ 85008-3410
- **Directions**: From the South on I-10: Take exit 143N, turn right on Washington, left on Priest Drive. Phoenix Municipal Stadium is on the corner of Van Buren and Priest. From the West: go on 202, north on Priest Drive. Phoenix Municipal Stadium is on the corner of Van Buren and Priest.

GCU BALLPARK

Grand Canyon University may be a relative newcomer in the world of major college baseball, but the program has a long history of success and a top-notch college facility in the form of GCU Ballpark on the Phoenix campus.

It is a ballpark that compares favorably to other ballparks in the spring-training-heavy Phoenix area, as well as other upper-level NCAA ballparks. GCU Ballpark features chair-back seating, a larger press box, an impressive concession stand with unique offerings (food items, like churros, served in team colors), an entertainment deck that can be adapted for multiple kinds of events, a pro-level sound system, new batting cages, and an upper-level concourse featuring great views of the mountain landscape. There are plenty of established Division I schools that would consider GCU Ballpark a significant upgrade. (No suites, alas.)

For fans, there are plenty of discrete places to take in a game, all designed to appeal to different constituencies. For students who are more casual fans, four-top seating on the upper level where homework and robust WiFi is as important as the cleanup batter. For families, a large deck down the right-field line featuring lots of table seating, kids' amusements, a food rail and bar-stool seating, and a large berm area for the kids to burn off some energy. For student superfans: plenty of room for the Havocs, who call themselves the rowdiest student section in the country. For everyone: plenty of shade and ceiling fans on both levels.

Like Arizona State, GCU schedules plenty of night games, and the team plays a very competitive schedule, with some top-rated team making the run to Phoenix. With the proximity to American Family Fields of Phoenix and the western training sites, you could put together a pleasant doubleheader combining a Cactus League match in the afternoon and a GCU game in the afternoon.

QUICK FACTS

- **Capacity:** 3,500
- **Year Opened:** 1962; renovated in 2018
- **Dimensions:** 320L, 390LC, 375C, 380RC, 330R
- **Surface:** Grass
- **Local Airport:** Phoenix
- **Ticket Prices:** Free
- **Website:** *gculopes.com*
- **Address:** 5159 N. 35th Av., Phoenix, AZ 85019
- **Directions:** GCU Ballpark is north of the 35th Avenue / Camelback Road interchange. The easiest way to visit: park in ramps north of the ballpark and then walk over.

LAS VEGAS

A weekend series in Las Vegas is one of the more enjoyable spring-training traditions in the Cactus League. The number of spring-training games in Vegas has expanded in recent years, making it a desirable destination for an exhibition—even if you never make it to Arizona.

Las Vegas Ballpark is located in suburban Summerlin, a high-end planned community to the west of downtown Las Vegas with over 100,000 residents. The centerpiece to the community is Downtown Summerlin, a mixed-use development that includes restaurants, bars, and plenty of shopping. The new ballpark is part of this downtown construction. The location is a good one: next to the Red Rock Casino complex, the Vegas Golden Knights (NHL) practice facility, and a planned downtown district, Las Vegas Ballpark benefits from easy access from a nearby freeway, three major streets, and plenty of side streets. Parking is free.

In fact, the presence of the Knights practice facility affected the ballpark design, with the left-field concourse butting up against it. This configuration narrows the outfield concourse and provides for only two rows of seats perched high on the 14-foot-high home-run wall. Signage for sponsors, the largest scoreboard in the minors (3,930 square feet) and large LAS VEGAS BALLPARK lettering blocks the view of the Knights practice facility.

This design choice, while not necessarily a physically required one, lends an air of intimacy to the ballpark—one that totally works. Spend any time in Vegas, and you realize everything sprawls. The casinos sprawl. Communities sprawl. Shopping malls sprawl.

So the intimacy is a nice contrast to the Vegas experience. Although the ballpark is located in a developed part of Summerlin, there's still a lot of open land to the east and south, used mainly for parking. The ballpark design is vertical, however, and creates an enclosed feel to the ballpark, which sits on a 7.65-acre site. You'll get that feeling at any place in the 360-degree concourse.

That enclosed feel begins with the large grandstand,

sporting a sleek, modern design that feels either like an abstract old-fashioned jetliner with a broad wingspan, convention center, or an airport terminal, depending on your point of view. (We instantly thought jetliner.)

The wings of the grandstand club level extend far down the lines, encompassing a club in the middle, suites to each side and party decks at each end, featuring plenty of indoor/outdoor seating. Folks have outfield spots at the drink rails and patio furniture, perhaps ordering from the right-field bar from the swimming pool. From the suite level, the lights of Vegas flicker in the distance when daylight fades away. At the top of the grandstand: the press box and the required A/V control equipment.

Like any new ballpark, Las Vegas Ballpark is divided into neighborhoods. The grandstand seating is for hardcore baseball fans, with drink rails on the concourse. The grandstand overhang extends farther than normal over the seating, which affects the view from the back rows of seating and the drink rails. A large concession stand is in the left-field corner, along with some drink stands.

Right field is the family area, with plenty of spots for the parents and the kids. The Hangar Bar is a standalone bar and lounge in right field, adjoining the right-center swimming pool, directly in back of the bullpens. The Hangar Bar is surrounded by lounge seating—chairs, chaise lounges—as well as four tops. A large 50-capacity pool, complete with lounge chairs and 14 barstools in the water, is geared toward groups, and the Hangar Bar runs right against it, allowing pool patrons to order their drinks while standing in the water. (A Vegas thing, to be sure. The Tropicana, for instance, was noted for its poolside bars and blackjack tables in the water, allowing patrons to play gamble in the water.) Multiple TVs entertain fans who care more about other sporting events than what's happening on the field. For the kids, there's a

Wiffle-ball diamond, a large berm, and plenty of places to view what's happening in the home and visitor bullpens.

It's a five-hour drive from Sloan Park to Las Vegas Ballpark, or a short one-hour flight from Sky Harbor to McCarran. And a cheap, short flight at that: you can find round-trip fares beginning at $75 thanks to plenty of competition from inexpensive airlines like Southwest, Frontier, and Spirit. We expect fans will fly out in the morning, rent a car for the longish drive out to Las Vegas Ballpark, return to the airport after the game, and fly back to Phoenix in time for the late games in the NCAA basketball tournament.

Las Vegas Ballpark, 1650 S. Pavilion Center Dr., Las Vegas; 702/943-7200; **thelvballpark.com**.

WHERE TO STAY

Summerlin sports a wide variety of lodging, ranging from the JW Marriott Las Vegas Resort & Spa to chains like Hampton Inn to several outposts of the popular Station chain for locals. Located within a short walk of the ballpark: the Red Rock Resort & Hotel (*11011 W. Charleston Blvd., Las Vegas; 702/797-7777;* **redrockresort.com**). This is a high-end resort, to be sure, with a large spa and pool, plenty of restaurants and bars, and a large casino. You could do worse as a baseball fan to be holed up at Red Rock Resort and then take in a few spring-training exhibitions.

One challenge given the suburban location of Las Vegas Ballpark: How to best plan a trip that combine the best of Vegas with the relatively remote location of Las Vegas Ballpark. One of the reasons the Las Vegas Aviators have been successful is the team's focus on drawing fans from the west Vegas metro and the fast-growing Summerlin area.

But this won't help you unless you plan on renting a car and hunkering down near the ballpark. Indeed, we know many of you have established habits for the exhibition weekend that includes a stay in downtown Las Vegas or somewhere on the Strip. Our advice: Don't feel compelled to stay out in Summerlin. If your traditional trip includes a stay at the Golden Nugget or the Four Queens and a dinner at Hugo's Cellar, keep that tradition alive and take a rideshare or limo out to the ballgame. If you're a true sports fan and want to take in as much action as possible, downtown's adult-only Circa Resort features a huge sports book, billed as the largest in Vegas, as well as a betting window in the three-story Stadium Swim amphitheater. There are some who swear by downtown Las Vegas—mostly older folks who have been going there for decades—and there's a certain Rat Pack quality to the area as well, even if all the sportsbooks have been modernized and the days of hand-written odds on a whiteboard are long gone. Embrace your inner Dean Martin.

Or, given the huge number of hotel rooms in Vegas, there's always the option of staying at one of the huge resort hotels on the Strip—the Flamingo, Planet Hollywood, the Horseshoe (formerly Bally's), Caesars Palace—that don't cost an arm and a leg but still offer plenty of entertainment. It's Vegas, baby: make the trip a true event.

ALSO FROM AUGUST PUBLICATIONS

The Complete Guide to Spring Training 2025 / Florida
My 1961
The Right Thing to Do: The True Pioneers of College Football Integration
Home Runs: Tales of Tonks, Taters, Contests and Derbies
The Baseball Thesaurus, 3e
The Football Thesaurus, 2e
Cradle of the Game: North Carolina Baseball Past and Present
Raye of Light: Jimmy Raye, Duffy Daugherty, The Integration of College Football, and the 1965-1966 Michigan State Spartans
Goodfellows: The Champions of St. Ambrose

Available from Amazon, Ingram, and augustpublications.com!